For Susan Christie,

who created
the right climate

THE CURSE OF AKKAD

CLIMATE UPHEAVALS THAT ROCKED HUMAN HISTORY

THE
CURSE
OF AKKAD

PETER CHRISTIE

annick press
toronto + new york + vancouver

Annick Press Ltd.

Edited by Elizabeth McLean
Proofread by Audrey McClellan
Cover and interior design by Irvin Cheung / iCheung Design, inc.
Cover illustrations: Clouds © istockphoto.com/Artur Achtelik; lightning ©
istockphoto.com/Scott Meeler; icicles © istockphoto.com/Slavoljub Pantelic; fall of
Babylon, from *L'Histoire du Vieux et du Nouveau Testament,* used by permission of Pitts
Theology Library.

We acknowledge the support of the Canada Council for the Arts, the Ontario Arts
Council, and the Government of Canada through the Book Publishing Industry
Development Program (BPIDP) for our publishing activities.

 ONTARIO ARTS COUNCIL
CONSEIL DES ARTS DE L'ONTARIO

Cataloguing in Publication
Christie, Peter, 1962-
    The curse of Akkad : climate upheavals that rocked human
history / Peter Christie.

Includes bibliographical references and index.
ISBN 978-1-55451-118-1 (pbk.).—ISBN 978-1-55451-119-8 (bound)

    1. Climate and civilization—History—Juvenile literature. 2. Climatic
changes—History—Juvenile literature. I. Title.
QC981.3.C52 2008   j551.609   C2007-907325-5

Printed and bound in Canada

Published in the U.S.A. by   **Distributed in Canada by**   **Distributed in the U.S.A. by**
Annick Press (U.S.) Ltd.   Firefly Books Ltd.   Firefly Books (U.S.) Inc.
                           66 Leek Crescent   P.O. Box 1338
                           Richmond Hill, ON   Ellicott Station
                           L4B 1H1   Buffalo, NY 14205

Visit our website at **www.annickpress.com**

CONTENTS

TODAY'S FORECAST

SIEGE OF THE SEA

As a child, Diana Wrightson loved to watch the sea. Now, many years later, she is the elderly owner of a quaint, seaside guest house—but she can only wring her hands when she sees the waves. One day soon, she says, the tossing sea will swallow up her English inn.

Diana lives in Happisburgh, England, northeast of London, and the waves of the North Sea have been washing away at the shore of her small village, bit by bit, for centuries.

In the past three decades, however, it has gotten much worse. A changing climate means the sea is rising—and waves are biting off bigger and bigger chunks of land. More than 10 meters (about 30 feet) of Happisburgh's sandy shoreline is lost to the water each year. The guest house, which is no longer open to guests, is now less than a car length from the hungry sea.

"The next big storm could take us away," Diana says sadly. "We're living on borrowed time."

Beautiful views of the North Sea made Diana Wrightson's guest house an ideal getaway before rising water levels threatened to wash it away.

Scientists say that global warming is melting glaciers and sea ice at the north and south poles, increasing the amount of water in the oceans. Higher temperatures also mean warmer water—and warm water expands to take up more space. Because of these changes, shorelines around the world are losing ground.

In Happisburgh, the news is bad. Since 1990, when a wooden seawall broke and left the shore unprotected, about 25 of the village's homes have simply fallen into the sea. Around the world, communities that live beside the ocean are under threat.

In Shishmaref, Alaska, not far from the Arctic Circle, the entire village of 600 people is leaving the island their ancestors have seasonally called home for more than 4000 years. A ring of ice used to arrive every year to protect their island from waves during the stormiest seasons. But the warmer climate means the ice doesn't come as early or grow as thick. Their village is being chewed to pieces by wild, rising seas.

ICE-LESS IN THE ARCTIC

The planet's white cap is shrinking. Satellite pictures show that the arctic ice cap is melting fast—so fast that arctic waters could be ice free by the time most 12-year-old kids have become 35-year-old adults.

Every year, the icy sheet that covers the top of the world shrinks in the summer heat before growing again in the winter. But in recent summers, this sheet has been smaller than ever. In the summer of 2007, for instance, the ice cap shrank by an area equal to about six Californias—to just over half its usual summer size.

The story may be similar at the planet's bottom. Water from the melting ice sheet that covers Antarctica is pouring into the sea at a yearly rate equal to all the water used by the United States, and its more than 300 million people, every three months.

An iceberg drifts near Antarctica. The amount of ice melting from the southern continent's glacier could fill as many as 60 million Olympic swimming pools every year.

In the South Pacific, other islanders are leaving, too. They're abandoning homes where they've lived for generations on the tiny Carteret atolls of Papua New Guinea. Waves now frequently wash over the low-lying islands, battering homes and destroying the coconut trees that the islanders grow. In 15 years, the islands will be completely under water.

Forced away by the sea, villagers along the coast from England to Alaska and the far-off South Pacific will soon be among the first refugees of present-day global warming. A part of their story, however, is familiar. Over 4000 years ago, a scribe told a tragic tale, carved into dusty clay tablets.

The ancient script on the tablets describes the curse of Akkad—and how an angry sky god was blamed for destroying the world's first empire. Akkad's citizens fled from a deadly drought that continued for decades, perhaps even for centuries, and its great cities were swallowed by dust and sand.

Researchers now believe "The Curse of Akkad" may be an account of ancient climate change.

CLIMATE THE ACTOR

Today, the old tale has a new and different spin. Everyone knows the climate is changing. We see it on the Internet, in books, and on TV. For the past century or more, our air and oceans have been getting warmer, and their temperatures are expected to rise even more.

What fewer people realize is that, although global warming is a special and severe case, climate change is not new. Sometimes slowly and sometimes quickly, seesawing between warm and cold, wet and dry, climate has always been on the move.

If human history were a (very long) school play, climate wouldn't be—as many of us might imagine—a backdrop of painted scenery. It would be an actor in the show. It would be doing things that influence the plot of the play.

And it would be onstage a lot.

Climate, of course, never acts alone. The cast of actors that has helped transform human societies includes wars, disease, technology, chance, and many others. But science is finding

EXTINCTION BLUES

For polar bears, the heat is on. Some researchers believe that the population of the white bears will drop by two-thirds within the next 45 years or so. Only 22,000 of the arctic bears live in the wild today, and the sea ice they travel over for hunting is disappearing fast.

While polar bears are unlikely to become extinct as long as summer sea ice remains in northern Greenland and elsewhere in the very high Arctic, other plants and animals may not be so lucky.

According to researchers, for each degree Celsius that the planet warms, plants and animals in the top half of the world have to shift their range northward by about 160 kilometers (100 miles) to survive. This may not sound very far for bigger animals or birds, but for plants, insects, and other small organisms that are part of the food chain this distance is vast. If— as many predict—the world becomes warmer by 3° Celsius (5.4° Fahrenheit) within the next 100 years, many species simply won't be able to make the long move.

Climate evidence from the distant past suggests that temperature changes of about 5° Celsius (9° Fahrenheit) have triggered mass extinctions that wiped out between 50 and 90 percent of all living things.

As arctic sea ice shrinks, polar bears could disappear from Alaska within the next 45 years.

The yearly rise in sea levels is measured in tenths of millimeters (small fractions of an inch), but little changes are causing big losses of shoreline.

more evidence that climate has often been near center stage for major events.

Climate is an important part of our lives. For instance, since humans began farming some 12,000 years ago, climate has determined where and when we can grow our food. It told us when to expect rain, when to sow seeds, and when to harvest.

But climate, for all its size and power, is a delicate thing. Many things influence it—the brightness of the sun, the orbit and tilt of the Earth, the activity of volcanoes, the size of the polar ice caps, the currents in the oceans, the winds in the air, and especially the gases in the atmosphere.

A change in the climate can bring too much water or not enough. It can make a place too hot or too cold. When crops don't grow or when food and water can't be found, people have to move—or die.

CLIMATE AND NOAH'S FLOOD

Like "The Curse of Akkad," the ancient story of Noah's flood—a story that appears in different forms in different cultures—may be based on a climate calamity.

After the end of the last great global cold snap, around 15,000 years ago, the world's oceans were filling to the brim with meltwater from glaciers. Sometime around 5650 BCE, the rising Mediterranean Sea burst through a natural dam in the Bosporus Valley of Turkey and flooded the Black Sea basin in a tremendous gush.

Salt water drowned everything in its path and transformed the freshwater lake that existed in the basin into a far larger, briny sea. Scientists say that many of the people who lived around the lake were likely lost in the flood. Those who escaped may have moved to the eastern Mediterranean or as far away as China—taking the tale of the great flood along with them.

Noah's Ark may be the best known, but tales of a great flood sent by God to punish people occur in ancient Hindu, Babylonian, and Greek traditions.

If climate has always changed, then why is it suddenly all over the news? It's because this time it's different. The climate is changing faster now than it has in the past 10,000 years. And, for the first time, people are behind it.

By burning fuels to power our homes, our factories, and our cars, we humans are creating carbon dioxide and other gases and dumping them into the sky. At the same time, we're clearing land to make farms and build cities, and we're destroying the forests that suck carbon dioxide back out of the air. The gases we spew and the forests we cut are changing our atmosphere so that it traps more heat from the sun. Our planet is heating up at an ever faster rate.

No one knows exactly what will happen. Many experts agree, however, that the scale of the climate upheaval we're facing has never been seen by civilized humans before. To cope with it, we'll need to keep our minds on the future. Thinking back to the past can be useful, too.

Although nature—not people—has been behind climate crises that struck earlier civilizations, we can still learn from our ancestors. Their stories can reveal what went right and what went wrong as cultures either flourished or died away during periods of abrupt change.

Our species has seen plenty of turbulent times. We've figured out how to adapt and survive. There may be lessons in our stormy history to help us face our new climate of change.

BEGINNINGS:
MOTHER ICE

THE STRANGERS

The girl had lived through eight summers when she saw the strangers for the first time. She spotted them early on a bright blue morning, while she sat on the ledge of a high limestone cliff. Although she knew they wouldn't see her, she crept to the shadows of a nearby cave. The group of lanky, odd-looking men was far below on a grassy plain. The girl, with an eagle's view from the cliff, stared in amazement.

She knew she should tell her parents. They were sleeping not far away, deeper within the cavern. But the sight of the strangers held the girl mesmerized and she couldn't look away.

The distant figures were running behind a small herd of deer, chasing them into a river. When the water slowed the panicked animals, the men moved in with spears and clubs. Others in the frigid water downstream waited for the floating and wounded deer.

The girl watched as the hunters jabbed furiously with their spears. Deer reared and tried to lunge to shore. Seen

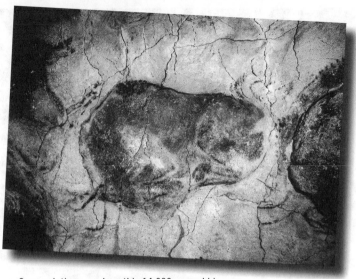

Cave paintings, such as this 14,000-year-old image
of a bison discovered at Altamira in Spain, show
some of the animals hunted by prehistoric humans.

from the cliff, the attack was a frenzy of splashing and blood.
But it was well organized, and by its end five deer lay dead
on the riverbank.

The men rested briefly and then began butchering their
kill, using sharpened stones. When they were finished, they
tied the deer to poles. A moment later, they carried them
into the trees.

The girl on the cliff could not make sense of what she'd witnessed.
The hunters weren't simply strangers. They were covered in
strange clothes and carried strange weapons. They hunted the
deer with a skill and speed that the girl had not seen before.

When she finally broke from her trance and ran to wake
the others, the girl gestured frantically. She brought her parents
and cousins to the cave mouth, but there was nothing to see.
Only a patch of bloodied grass remained at the riverside. The
strangers had disappeared.

A TOOL FOR ALL TIME

Never mind the cell phone or the computer. The most important tool in human history was the stone hand axe. Nicknamed the Swiss Army knife of prehistoric times, the hand axe was such a great thingamajig that it remained the tool of choice for more than 1.5 million years.

The axe was an oval or triangular piece of stone that people sharpened by chipping off flakes around its edges. It was used for cutting, splitting, hacking, and slicing everything from food to trees. But it may have been invented for another purpose.

Scientists believe the first hand axe was made by *Homo erectus* about 1.8 million years ago. Africa at the time was often dry, and water holes were scarce. Animals were forced to crowd together to drink.

The axe shape is good for throwing, and it orients in the air with its sharp edges forward. Thrown into a crowded herd, the axe could have wounded an animal so hunters could move in for the kill. The theory is controversial, but it explains why so many of these axes turn up beside ancient watering holes.

Stone hand axes like this one have been found across large areas of Africa, Europe, and Asia.

The Neanderthal girl would never fully understand what she'd seen—the strange hunters were modern humans. For a quarter of a million years, the Neanderthals had ruled Europe uncontested. The arrival of modern humans was about to change that. Soon, the world of the Neanderthals would be turned upside down.

INTRODUCED BY CLIMATE This imagined scene likely never took place, but it might have. Until as recently as 24,000 years ago, the last known Neanderthal home was a cliff-side cavern known as Gorham's Cave on the Rock of Gibraltar near Spain. The cave overlooked a vast, marshy plain that's now lost beneath the Mediterranean Sea.

No one knows whether the people we call Neanderthals (*Homo neanderthalensis*—sometimes called *Homo sapiens neanderthalensis*) and modern humans (*Homo sapiens*) ever met or even saw each other, but many scientists suspect they did. They may have been introduced by climate change.

For more than 100,000 years, our species and the Neanderthals—our closest relatives—likely lived entirely unaware of each other. Despite sharing a common ancestor (*Homo erectus*), the Neanderthals evolved and thrived in Europe and Asia, while our species evolved and flourished in Africa.

Then the cold came. The last big global deep freeze took place between about 118,000 and 15,000 years ago. That's when huge sheets of ice—glaciers—began crawling south, deep into Europe.

Homo sapiens had been living comfortably in many parts of Africa, including its dry, grassy northern plains. But the expanding glaciers were sucking up the world's water, and the

The Rock of Gibraltar (pictured here) is the site of Gorham's Cave. Artifacts suggest that Neanderthals survived there until as recently as 24,000 years ago.

climate was changing. Some places, including northern Africa, turned dry — becoming what is now the Sahara Desert.

People were pushed to the outer fringes of the desert. From there, many went north into Europe. They arrived as the advancing northern ice pressed the Neanderthals into southern Europe as well.

THE LAST ONES STANDING

Scientists believe *Homo sapiens* appeared in Europe about 40,000 years ago. That would mean they lived alongside their ancient cousins for as long as 16,000 years before the last known Neanderthals disappeared from Gibraltar.

Many also believe the meeting of these two peoples could help explain why the Neanderthals vanished. *Homo sapiens* had better hunting equipment, including harpoons, complex tools, and possibly even fishing nets. They were able to sew clothes with a bone needle, giving better protection from the cold.

DRILLING INTO THE CLIMATE'S PAST

Did a changing climate help make us who we are? Scientists may be getting closer to an answer, thanks to techniques that tell us what the climate was like when our human ancestors were evolving.

One tool is long thin columns—or cores—drilled from the ocean bottom or from glaciers. The cores show bands along their length that correspond to the layers of mud or snow that settled there in the distant past.

The layers trap and preserve ancient climate markers. From cores extracted out of the seafloor, scientists can analyze the fossil remains of microscopic sea animals. These reveal information about temperature and dryness at the time these animals lived—as far back as 70 million years ago.

This core of ice from almost 2 kilometers (1.2 miles) deep in a Greenland glacier shows bands of ice, dust, and chemicals from the air that settled there over 16,000 years ago.

The layers in ice cores trap telltale chemicals from the air as well as dust and material that settled on glaciers long ago. In 2000, an ice core 3.5 kilometers (2 miles) long was pulled from the ice sheet in Antarctica. It tells a climate story going back 420,000 years.

The Neanderthals may have been outsmarted (although a few scientists dispute this theory). It's possible that the more sophisticated modern humans simply won out in the struggle for food and space, or that they even killed the Neanderthals they met.

Whatever happened, the outcome is clear: ours became the only human species left on Earth.

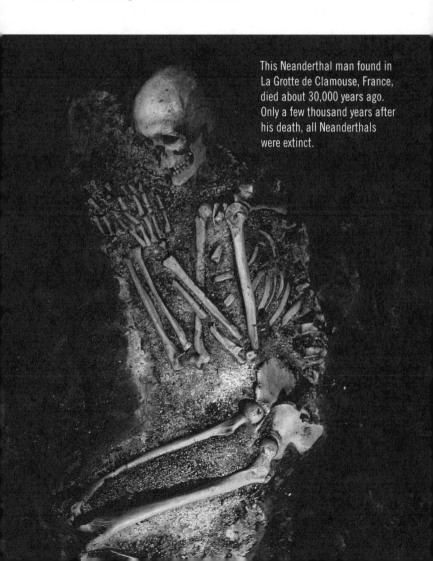

This Neanderthal man found in La Grotte de Clamouse, France, died about 30,000 years ago. Only a few thousand years after his death, all Neanderthals were extinct.

Outlasting the Neanderthals is just one part of the prehistoric drama that helped make us who we are. It's a drama that has long puzzled scientists, and many theories exist to explain why it played out the way it did.

Only recently, however, have researchers begun to focus on a revealing coincidence. Many of the most important episodes of human evolution and change occurred when climate was changing as well—during the last great ice age.

PLANET OF THE APES

The last ice age was well underway during the time of our ape ancestors. Today, there are few ape species (among them gorillas, orangutans, chimpanzees, and gibbons), and many of these are endangered. But back between 22 and 5.5 million years ago—still millions of years before the first humans—apes were the champions of the world. As many as 100 different species lived and roamed across much of Africa, Europe, and Asia.

So which of these apes was the great-grand-ape to humans? According to new research, it was probably an ape living in Europe or Asia—not in Africa, as many people think.

Although the earliest apes emerged in Africa, some left and became jungle royalty elsewhere. By about 16 million years ago, they were at home in Europe and Asia.

A few million years later, the developing ice age altered the world around them. The near-tropical climate of Europe turned cold. In Asia, forests dried into scattered woodlands and grasslands. Deserts formed. Many apes became extinct.

Only two ancient Eurasian ape lineages managed to escape. They were big-brained apes, capable of finding new foods in a changing environment. Moving south ahead of the cold, they

FROZEN IN TIME

Ice ages are times when the Earth has been home to large and lasting glaciers. The most recent one began about 40 million years ago, but it didn't really hit its stride until many millions of years later. That's when glaciers formed across much of the north as well as in the southern part of the planet. It was a time of climate shifts, migration, and evolutionary change.

Although technically, the last ice age is still going on—the north and south poles are still covered by ice sheets—most consider that the ice age ended when

When the global climate shifts into ice-age cold, massive glaciers grow around the world.

the last glaciers retreated from much of North America, Europe, and Asia about 15,000 years ago.

survived. One of these ape lines fled to southeast Asia. It was probably an early ancestor of the orangutans that still live in Borneo and Indonesia.

The other returned to Africa about 9 million years ago. There, luckily for us, it stuck around and put down the roots of what became the human family tree.

Gorillas and other large apes can travel quickly over land on their knuckles.

But a funny thing happened on the way to the jungle.

As the climate in Europe and Asia became colder and drier, the forests shrank as the apes slowly migrated south. There were fewer trees for them to swing through in their usual style of traveling.

According to some researchers, the need to move across open territory may explain why some of these apes evolved the ability to walk on the ground using their hind feet and their front knuckles.

"Knuckle walking" is used today by chimpanzees, gorillas, and orangutans. It's a trick that allows the apes to travel faster across open ground. It's also a trick that may mark the first step in the evolution of walking upright on two feet.

WOBBLING THROUGH SPACE

Glaciers have bulldozed across the landscape whenever the world was gripped by a big chill. The cause of these periodic deep freezes—ice ages—may have something to do with Earth's wobbly path through space.

When our planet goes around the sun each year, the shape of the route is a bit oval, or elliptical, not perfectly circular. Meanwhile, the planet spins on a slightly tilted axis—the imaginary line through the north and south poles.

Earth's orbit gets a little rounder or more oval every 100,000 years or so. Over periods of about 41,000 years, the planet's axis alters, too, so that the spinning Earth wobbles, like a top. During cycles of 22,000 years, our orbit alters the time of year when our globe is closest to the sun.

All of this can cause long-lasting shifts in the world's climate.

Sometimes the north pole tilts farther toward deep, cold outer space at the same time the planet is at its farthest from the sun. Cold winters follow year after year, ice sheets begin to grow, and the great glacial bulldozers rumble to life.

Small changes to the Earth's tilt and its orbit around the sun can cause big, long-term alterations in our climate.

A JACK OF ALL TRADES

The ice age continued, and so did evolution. About 3 million years ago, the first northern glaciers of the ice age appeared, and the climate became more and more unstable.

For tens of thousands of years at a time, icy glaciers rolled forward and backward over the top of the planet like frigid bulldozers. The massive ice sheets pushed south into Europe, Asia, and North America, freezing and often crushing any life in the way. Eventually, they would retreat, only to advance again thousands of years later.

THE JANITOR GENIUS

James Croll of Scotland was an unlikely scientific hero. In 1864, while working as a "keeper," or custodian, at a Scottish museum, he first proposed that the Earth's orbit may have caused the ice ages.

The idea changed science, and now it is widely accepted. But Croll wasn't a trained scientist. He had no schooling after the age of 13 and spent most of his life moving from job to job. He worked as a carpenter, a hotel operator, and an insurance agent. He even ran a tea shop for a while.

Finally, Croll landed work as a museum janitor. It gave him time to write, and he began sending his scientific ideas to journals. They made him famous, and he was soon given work with the geological survey of Scotland. The self-taught genius went on to write two scientific books and 87 scientific papers before he died in 1890.

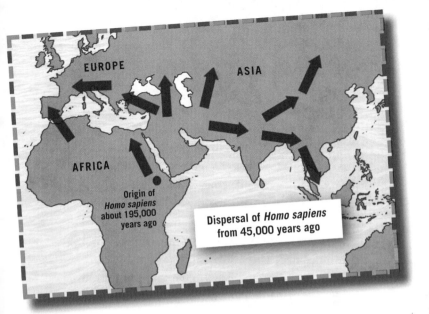

EUROPE

ASIA

AFRICA

Origin of
Homo sapiens
about 195,000
years ago

Dispersal of *Homo sapiens*
from 45,000 years ago

The northern glaciers appeared as *Homo erectus* began to evolve in eastern Africa.

Many believe this early ancestor of both Neanderthals and *Homo sapiens* evolved between about 2.5 and 1.9 million years ago. According to some scientists, the restless climate of the time may have helped *Homo erectus* get a head start in the race for survival.

Their big advantage was brainpower. The climate in east Africa was causing massive changes to the plants and animals that lived there. It was a drier, less forested place where antelope and wild pigs grazed. These beasts migrated and evolved with the changing environment. Fossils show that the plant life was also in a state of flux.

***Homo erectus* found that** it could use its brain to cope with the topsy-turvy climate.

At the time, *Homo erectus* shared the planet with other descendants of the human-like apes called Australopiths.

Members of one such group, *Paranthropus*, were specialists capable of munching up the tougher plants of a drier world. But our ancestors hedged their bets and learned to eat a lot of different things.

The strategy required thinking—they had to discover the tricks of finding food in a changing world. But it worked. While *Paranthropus* disappeared about a million years ago, *Homo erectus* survived. In time, *Homo erectus* gave rise to the Neanderthals and, later, to a different branch—our own species.

Although brainiac *Homo sapiens* didn't make their appearance until about 195,000 years ago, our *Homo erectus* ancestors firmly committed us to the path of using our superior brainpower to get along in a changing world.

DROUGHT! THE CURSE OF AKKAD

Under the hot sun, the boy strained against the rope. Enkidu was not yet 14, but he was proud of his strength. Born into a laboring family, he had no recollection of a time before hard work.

The others called him Enkidu after the wild man character in an old story of an ancient king; Enkidu in the tale was powerful, too.

The year was 2200 BCE. Enkidu was one of many boys and men who were hauling huge black blocks of basalt rock using only ropes and pulleys. They were dragging them from a quarry, far across fields, to the city of Shekhna. Their backs bare to the sun, they sweated as they inched the rocks forward. The rising wind provided no cool relief. It was hot, too, and only blew dust into their faces from the dry fields.

The blocks would become part of a new government building in the city. Surrounded by fields of grain, Shekhna was an

DUSTY CLUES TO THE AKKAD FAILURE

Researchers suspect that climate was involved in the death of the city of Shekhna because of a thick blanket of dust and sand covering the ruins.

The deep sand suggested that the ground around the city became so dry the wind could blow it about freely. And earthworms, which need moist dirt to survive, all died away at about the same time.

Another clue was discovered to the southeast, in the Gulf of Oman. The amount of dust that had settled on the seafloor, carried from Mesopotamia by the wind, increased by 500 percent beginning abruptly in the century leading up to 2200 BCE. Normal levels did not return for centuries.

important northern outpost in the kingdom of Akkad—the world's first empire.

The empire had been created a century earlier by Sargon of Akkad, an apprentice gardener from the city-kingdom of Kish, who rose to power and then conquered one neighboring city after another. Sargon had taken control of great areas of farmland and built fortresses to protect the grain. The center of his empire was the city of Akkad, but his rule spread across Mesopotamia (roughly modern-day Iraq) and beyond.

His grandson, Naram-sin, now ruled the empire. Enormous buildings, including the one planned for Shekhna, were being built as monuments to Akkadian greatness. Workers such as Enkidu were paid in rations of barley and oil.

But Enkidu felt uneasy. Rations had been poor lately, and many of the workers were growing sick from hunger. Around them, people in the city were desperate, too. Many were leaving to search for food in the countryside.

"Enlil," said Enkidu.

His friends looked anxiously up at the fierce sun—there had been little rain in many months. Enkidu told them the news he had heard. Emperor Naram-sin had attacked a temple built to honor the sky god, called Enlil. Naram-sin had become enraged when two of the temple's soothsayers predicted that his luck would turn bad.

"The lord of the sky is angry," Enkidu concluded ominously.

Not long after, work stopped altogether. The blocks that had been painstakingly hauled to the site sat unused. A wall stood partially complete. Chisels and hammers were abandoned. As Enkidu and the other workers left the site, the rest of the people abandoned the city. Everyone, it seems, was moving to save their lives.

Sargon of Akkad, who called himself "king of the world," ruled the vast empire he created for 56 years.

DRIED TO DUST

In the 1980s, researchers uncovered the remains of Shekhna at a site that is now called Tell Leilan, in the remote plains of northeastern Syria. From under waist-high sand drifts, they found the unfinished wall. The details of Enkidu's story are imagined, but scientists found evidence that people emptied the city in a hurry.

At least part of the reason appears to have been climate disaster. About 4200 years ago, the Akkad empire was hit by a massive drought accompanied by strong winds. The layers of sand and dust that settled over Shekhna after it was abandoned show a dry period that began quickly and lasted for as long as 300 years.

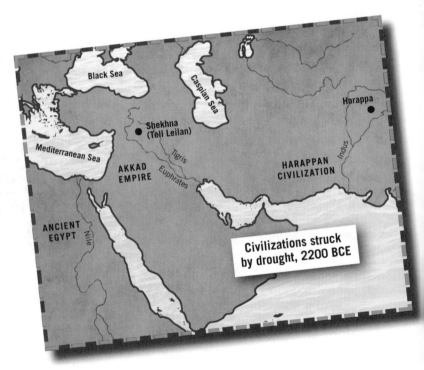

Civilizations struck by drought, 2200 BCE

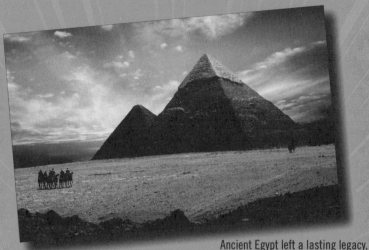

THE LOST CIVILIZATION

Ancient Egypt left a lasting legacy, including the Great Pyramids. The Harappan civilization, which thrived at about the same time, seemed to disappear from history.

Early human civilizations in Egypt, Mesopotamia, and China had a powerful influence on the cultures that followed. But the Harappan civilization has a different story—it vanished almost without a trace.

Often called the "lost civilization," Harappan society thrived in the Indus Valley in what is now Pakistan at about the same time ancient Egypt was flourishing. As in Egypt, Harappan people lived by a great river. They counted on the Indus's annual floods for good crops year after year. Like Egypt's, the Harappan civilization was complex: it had its own writing system and made buildings using the world's first oven-fired bricks. Also like Egypt, the Harappan civilization failed around 2200 BCE, probably destroyed by the same crop-killing drought.

Unlike Egypt, however, the Harappan civilization crumbled into dust so completely that it all but disappeared from history.

Without enough water for crops, the entire kingdom suffered. As people starved or moved, the empire disintegrated.

An account of the disaster was unearthed by archeologists. The poem, written on clay tablets less than a century after the event, was called "The Curse of Akkad":

> The large fields and acres produced no grain.
> The flooded fields produced no fish.
> The watered gardens produced no honey and wine.
> The heavy clouds did not rain.
> On its plains where grew fine plants,
> lamentation reeds now grow.

The soothsayers' prediction had come true. Drought apparently helped defeat the empire built by Sargon of Akkad. It was not the only time that a drier climate played a part when an early civilization collapsed into ruin.

"THIS SANDBANK OF HELL"

As a district chief in the southern region of ancient Egypt, Ankhtifi was like any city official: he worked to collect taxes and grain and to keep the local government running smoothly. But everything changed in about 2185 BCE. That's when disaster struck, and Ankhtifi's main concern became simply keeping the people in his region alive: "I fed the people of my area at a time when the sky was in tumult and the land was in the wind and everyone was dying of hunger on this sandbank of Hell."

Ancient Egypt is perhaps the most famous early civilization. For more than a thousand years, Egypt's Old Kingdom—ruled by a succession of powerful pharaohs who saw themselves as

Ancient Egyptians used nilometers, often notches alongside stairs to the water, to determine Nile flood levels and the likelihood of drought.

gods—was one of the most important centers of food growing and culture in the ancient world.

It was the time of golden statues, hieroglyphs, eye-popping art, and cloth-wrapped mummies. It was also the time when the Egyptians built the Great Pyramids—one of the most amazing feats of human architecture of any time.

Then—while Ankhtifi watched—this great and ancient society tumbled into chaos.

"All of Upper Egypt was dying of hunger to such a degree that everyone had come to eating his children," reported Ankhtifi. His account of the time was later inscribed in his tomb. The district leader wanted to be remembered for helping his community survive when all around him was a devastating famine. "The entire country had become like a starved grasshopper, with people going to the north and to the south."

EGYPT'S RED MUD

One squishy but important clue to the mystery of ancient Egypt came from near the Nile River. It was a layer of red mud.

Researchers drilled a column of dirt from the Nile delta, where the river flows into the Mediterranean Sea.

In the layers upon layers of muck and silt, one was noticeably red. The age of the mud layer matched the time of Egypt's collapse.

The red was iron oxide, a mineral that becomes concentrated during long droughts. The researchers concluded that the flat plain around the Nile's delta went without much water for about 200 years.

The terrible drought of 2200 BCE affected Egypt in much the same way it destroyed the Akkad empire. The Nile River, which Egyptian farmers counted on to flood their fields during the seasonal rains, shrank for lack of water. Many researchers say that climate was behind it.

Ancient beach stones left far from water reveal shrinking shorelines, as lakes fed by the Nile almost completely dried up. For about 200 years, the low plains that were flooded by the Nile every year appeared to receive very little water. Dunes of sand began to cover the region's best farm fields.

The mighty pharaohs tried but failed to control their kingdom. Few crops grew, and food shortages were made worse by people who hoarded precious grain. Egyptians fought amongst themselves, desperate with hunger. It was, say some historians, the beginning of the first Dark Age.

Some Egyptian settlements recovered within a few decades, however. They discovered a way to get water to their crops by digging ditches from the Nile through their fields—a simple form of irrigation. But the rest of the kingdom continued to struggle for many years.

THE MYSTERY OF THE MAYAN COLLAPSE

Sometime after 900 CE, servants in the huge, stone palace at the center of the Mayan city of Calakmul were setting things in order. Everything—the massive ceramic jars, the stone tools, and the blades made from volcanic glass—was stored carefully away. The royal kitchen, with its cooking vessels and grinding stones, stood ready for the next meal. Yes, the royal household was leaving—like everyone else in the troubled city. But the palace dwellers expected to return.

It didn't work out that way. No one ever again lived in

Chac, whose image is carved on this sculpture in Mexico, was the Mayan god of rain and storms.

the palace, and Calakmul, one of the largest ancient Mayan cities, near the center of what is now Mexico's Yucatan Peninsula, stood empty for centuries. The palace and the city were completely abandoned sometime in the early 900s, among the last of the great Mayan city centers to be abruptly left behind by its people.

Why the centuries-old civilization of the ancient Mayans so quickly disappeared has long been a mystery. Between about 50 and 800 CE, the ancient Mayans built an impressive society in the lowlands and jungles of Central America. Their sophisticated culture of science, religion, and art depended on the hard work of farmers who harvested corn and other crops in fields outside the walls of their great city-kingdoms, such as Calakmul, Tikal, and Copán.

The Mayan rulers and priests collected and stored water in reservoirs and underground tanks, or cisterns, doling it out during the dry winter months. They built dams and canals, too, to carry water through the cities. A reliable supply of water was crucial to their survival. One of the Mayan traditions that may be hard for us to understand was their ritual human sacrifices. They believed that spilling human blood would please their rain god and ensure enough rainfall for good harvests.

CULTIVATED BY CLIMATE

Farming depends upon climate—and not just for weather that brings good harvests. As a way of life, farming may have been forced upon us by climate change.

Before about 12,000 years ago, a group of early hunter-gatherers known as the Natufian people lived by roaming in search of gazelle and wild plants across a large area of Asia near the eastern end of the Mediterranean Sea. The climate—warm and wet in the winter and hot and dry in the summer—supported wild grasses and grazing animals.

When a global cold snap occurred from 12,900 to 11,600 years ago, the Natufian hunting grounds became cool and dry. Many plant and animal species disappeared from the area.

The city of Jericho, site of a great battle in biblical times, was also home to the Natufian people thousands of years earlier. They planted crops in a nearby oasis.

To survive, the Natufians settled down and began growing edible grasses and other plants, and raising animals to eat. It was the birth of farming—and it changed the course of human civilization.

Beginning in the late eighth and early ninth centuries, the Mayan civilization began to disappear. At their peak, Mayan cities were home to tens of thousands of people, but within a few centuries they were abandoned, and the jungle took over. Cities, temples, and pyramids all vanished behind a thick shroud of trees.

Researchers have tried to solve the mystery for years. Some have blamed disease. Others have said that wars between city-states tore the society apart. Now, many scientists think climate change was partially responsible.

The ancient Mayans were accomplished artists and sculptors.

THE WHY OF DRY

No one knows for sure what caused many of the great droughts that have rocked human civilizations as far back as ancient Akkad, but research indicates that these climate changes were felt around the world.

The 2200 BCE drought affected Akkad and Egypt, as well as early civilizations in Greece and the Indus Valley. Evidence from seabeds and glacier ice shows that the dry climate reached from Ghana to Ethiopia in Africa, and as far away as Tibet and South America. Some scientists blame a regular 1450-year climate cycle that may be triggered by changes in the sun's energy or a shift in ocean currents.

Recently, researchers have linked the drought that affected both the ancient Mayans and the Tang Dynasty of China to a belt of moist air that typically circles the Earth at the equator. The seasonal movement of this belt makes the regions beneath it alternately wet or dry through the year. Scientists say that a long-term change in the position of this belt may have stuck these places in a dry cycle for centuries.

Beginning in about 760, the region became much drier, enduring a devastating series of droughts. Researchers say that the period between 800 and 1000 was the region's driest two centuries in 8000 years.

The timeline matches perfectly the decline and fall of the Mayan cities. Season after season, the summer rains failed, leaving crops without water and people without food.

HIGH AND DRY IN THE ANDES

Lake Titicaca, on the border of Bolivia and Peru, is unusual in many ways. At about 3.8 kilometers (12,500 feet) above sea level, it's the highest lake in the world big enough to sail a ship on. Its shores were also once home to an ancient, sprawling empire.

The Tiwanaku civilization began as a simple farming community in about 300 BCE and became very successful. Irrigated and terraced fields allowed farmers to grow crops despite the altitude and cold. Cities developed, and palaces were built with enormous sandstone blocks. By 700 CE, the influence of the empire's lakeside capital, the city of Tiwanaku, reached all the way to the Pacific Ocean.

Scientists believe the society fell apart beginning in about 1100. That's also about the time when summer rains began to dry up. Lake Titicaca shrank drastically. According to researchers, its water level may have dropped by as much as 10 meters (over 30 feet). The lake eventually recovered, but the Tiwanaku civilization could not.

Traditional reed boats like this one are believed to have been used during the centuries-old Tiwanaku civilization on Lake Titicaca.

Researchers believe the droughts devastated the corn crops—and cornbread was a staple food of the Mayans. Other vegetables and grains also failed to grow with very little water.

The idea that Mayan kings could influence the gods began to evaporate in the dry air. Crowds stared in disbelief as their rulers explained there was no water to give them.

Not long after, say historians, the Mayan people, weakened by hunger, were probably struck by disease. Wars between neighboring cities gathered a new and fierce momentum as they fought over reservoirs of water or stored corn and other foods. People fled or died by the thousands. And the magnificent Mayan culture disintegrated.

CHINA'S "GOOD RAIN" TURNS BAD

"The good rain knows its season," wrote the Chinese poet Du Fu. "When spring arrives, then it comes. It follows the wind secretly into the night."

Du Fu was one of the leading writers of a golden age of art and culture that flourished in China at around the same time the Mayan civilization was reaching its peak. This period in China, which began in 618, is known as the Tang Dynasty.

Much of China's history is divided according to dynasties—times when China was ruled by the same royal family. The Tang Dynasty, which lasted for almost three centuries, was among the greatest. Even today, the poetry from that time is thought to be some of the best China has ever produced.

As it did for the Mayans, the end came tragically. The Tang Dynasty faltered, then fell, and was followed by years of chaos. Many researchers say at least some of the blame belongs to a shifting climate.

Rice grows in flooded fields, or paddies, and strong seasonal rains are needed to produce a good harvest.

Not long after 760—about the same year Du Fu wrote his poem "Welcome Rain on a Spring Night"—the seasonal rains so vital to Chinese farms began to weaken. A series of droughts ravaged the countryside through the next century. Rice paddies dried into cracked earth. Farmers could only stare, helpless, as fruit and other crops failed in the heat and dust. Millions went hungry.

Research suggests that the worst of the dry periods occurred around 810, 860, and 910—the same years that rainless skies brought famine and ruin to the Mayans halfway around the world.

It was too much for the Tang Dynasty. A series of rebellions flared up, and the last Tang emperor was forced to abandon the throne. From a highly sophisticated society, China fell into decades of famine, wars, and cultural darkness.

THE MEDIEVAL WARM PERIOD: AN ADVENTUROUS WIND

LOST SAILORS, A FOUND WORLD

As Bjarni Herjolfsson boarded his ship, he thought the pale afternoon light of the western horizon looked menacing. The dark swells of the North Atlantic gently rocked the boat, anchored off the northern coast of Iceland.

"Our journey will be thought an ill-considered one," said Bjarni as his crew readied the sail, "since none of us has sailed the Greenland Sea."

Bjarni was probably not used to feeling uneasy. He was a Viking, after all. By his lifetime—the late 900s—Vikings had already established a reputation as fearless warriors and master sailors. Besides, Bjarni, a trader, was used to long journeys in his trustworthy ship.

But this was his first voyage to Greenland, and the ocean west of Iceland was notorious. Icebergs were common hazards, and the winds could turn deadly fierce, churning the sea into a maelstrom that could smash a ship into kindling.

Despite the dangers, Bjarni and his crew set sail. Bjarni's

Even for the Vikings' seaworthy longships, the voyage between Iceland and Greenland could be treacherous.

father had successfully made the journey and was living among the new colonies of Erik "the Red" Thorvaldsson. The Viking trader was determined to visit Greenland and to see his father.

For three days, Bjarni's ship sailed without incident. Then the wind dropped.

A fog settled over the ship like a funeral shroud. Bjarni could distinguish day from night, but nothing more. The stars and the sun—natural beacons that the Viking needed for navigation—were lost from view. The men sailed blindly over the cold gray sea.

Days passed before a morning sun finally burned through the haze. Thanking his Viking gods, Bjarni hoisted his sails. The wind picked up. By the end of the day, he spied land.

But something was wrong. Bjarni had never visited Greenland, but he had heard descriptions of its barren, mountainous coast. This shore was different. It was heavily

BRIGHTER SUN, WARMER DAYS

What turned up the heat during the Medieval Warm Period is a question without a clear answer. But scientists believe the sun actually shone brighter during those centuries.

This sunspot photo clearly shows a cold, dark area surrounded by a bright ring of fire.

A brighter sun means more solar energy hitting the Earth, resulting in warmer air. It's caused by an increase in the number of sunspots—dark spots on the sun's surface where the temperature is a few thousand degrees lower than usual. Surrounding each spot is a ring of intense fire, so the overall effect is brighter.

Although astronomers in China and Japan have counted visible sunspots since ancient times, highly accurate records didn't exist until the invention of the telescope in about 1610. To estimate solar activity before that, scientists use other clues.

Records of the northern lights (aurora borealis) and its southern cousin (aurora australis) exist far back in history. Frequent aurora displays are seen during periods of increased sunspots. Carbon found in the wood of trees provides another clue. Carbon atoms combine in different forms, depending on the intensity of the sun.

wooded, with no mountains. Hills sloped up from the sea, and clownish Atlantic puffins nested or swam by the thousands among rocky islets.

What land could this be? Realizing he was lost, Bjarni turned his ship northward. Sailing on, he and his crew passed more lands that bore no resemblance to Greenland. With each day, the men became more afraid they would never see familiar shores or faces again.

Four long days after losing sight of another inhospitable coast, Bjarni saw land once more. It rose from the sea like the bald mound of a grave rising from the earth. Windswept and barren, the coast seemed eerily silent. Never would Bjarni have imagined that such a bleak sight could make him feel so glad.

"This land is most like what I have been told of Greenland," he said. "We'll head to shore here."

LEIF ERIKSSON'S STORY

We know about Bjarni's harrowing voyage from an account written in Iceland about 600 years ago. The story had been passed down from sailor to sailor for generations before it was finally recorded in a text called *Greenlanders' Saga*.

The importance of the tale is clear. Before he reached the Greenland colonies, Bjarni had been blown to the coast of North America. A lost Viking had come upon the New World about 500 years before Spanish explorer Christopher Columbus laid claim to the discovery.

The story Bjarni told when he reached Greenland inspired Erik the Red's son, Leif Eriksson. A few years later, Leif attempted to retrace Bjarni's route, and in about 1000, he sailed into a wooded bay midway along the coast of what is now Labrador, in Canada.

CLIMATE'S ROBIN HOOD

Did the Medieval Warm Period make a hero of Robin Hood? Some researchers say it's possible.

Many believe the legend of Robin Hood—an outlaw hero who defied an evil king and lived in the forest—is based on the real-life exploits of a daring English rebel called Hereward the Wake. Hereward led a band of men who fought against Norman rule after William the Conqueror invaded England from Normandy in 1066.

Hereward's base was the Isle of Ely. Today, Ely is a coastal city about a two-hour drive north of London, but back then it was an island surrounded by marshes. The Medieval Warm Period caused glaciers and ice sheets to melt, raising sea levels around the world and flooding the area around Ely.

The channels, marshes, and forested islets provided the perfect hideout for Hereward and his band. Hereward's fate is unknown, but some sources suggest he may have made peace with the king and, like the Robin Hood of legend, lived lawfully ever after.

Like the legendary Robin Hood, Hereward the Wake became known for his cleverness and daring.

Leif Eriksson, the descendant of outlaw explorers, was likely the first European to explore the New World.

Leif stepped ashore, delighted by the abundance of timber—badly needed for building on the sparsely treed shores of Greenland. And he became the first European known to have set foot in North America.

Leif's achievement capped more than a century of Viking adventure in the North Atlantic.

Iceland had been settled in the 870s. A century later, about 985, Erik the Red had pioneered the colonies of Greenland. (Legend has it that Erik,

A CATHEDRAL CLIMATE

Europeans had a lot to be thankful for during the Medieval Warm Period. Despite the occasional war, and raids by Viking marauders, the people of Europe enjoyed a long period when crops grew tall and few went hungry.

Gratitude and prosperity help to explain why architects and masons in Europe's cities became swept up in a tide of church building. Several of the greatest cathedrals in history were built during this period, including the vast Canterbury Cathedral in England. It was rebuilt, beginning in 1070, after a major fire. In Paris, work a hot-headed renegade who was banished from Iceland for murder, enticed other colonists to follow him by telling them tales of a great "green land," perfect for cattle farming.) Then his son Leif pushed the Vikings' westward expansion all the way to the Americas.

Leif and his relatives explored down the North American coast, possibly as far south as Maine, and inland along the St. Lawrence River. They even established a settlement for a few years—the ruins of eight Viking buildings were found at L'Anse aux Meadows in Newfoundland.

Canterbury Cathedral is one of the oldest and most celebrated Christian buildings in England.

on the magnificent Notre Dame cathedral began in 1159, though the church was not finished for another 200 years. The cathedral of Notre Dame de Chartres in northern France was erected in 1195—a classic example of the towering, gothic style of the time.

Viking explorations

GREENLAND
ICELAND
SCANDINAVIA
Atlantic Ocean
NORTH AMERICA
L'Anse aux Meadows
EUROPE

····· Viking settlement of Iceland, 870s
--- Erik "the Red" Thorvaldsson, about 985
—— Bjarni Herjolfsson, about 986
······ Leif Eriksson, about 1000

Viking outposts stretched halfway around the top of the world, from the mouth of the St. Lawrence to the ports of northern Europe. Good boats, fearlessness, and a lack of farmland at home encouraged their explorations. Squeezed out of their Scandinavian homelands, the Vikings were looking for new land to farm and better lives.

Climate, say researchers, was another important player in this drama. The Vikings became the world's most adventurous seafaring people at the time that Europe and North America were experiencing a remarkable, extended warm spell, now known as the Medieval Warm Period.

Between 800 and 1300, scientists say average temperatures in many parts of the world were higher than they had been for the previous 8000 years. The warmer climate broke up sea ice that would have made the Viking voyages impossible. It also made Greenland winters bearable and crops possible.

Paddling in open, outrigger canoes, Polynesian explorers settled remote Pacific islands, such as Easter Island and Hawaii.

PADDLING TO THE EDGE OF THE EARTH

The Vikings were not the only group to become bold explorers during the Medieval Warm Period.

On the other side of the planet, the Polynesian people of the South Pacific also took to the open sea. With only hand-carved paddles and simple outrigger canoes, the Polynesians made dangerous ocean voyages of as much as 2900 kilometers (1800 miles), all the way to New Zealand.

The Polynesians had achieved the first of their remarkable feats of seamanship almost 2000 years earlier. Sailing from eastern Indonesia without navigational instruments, they had arrived in Fiji, Tonga, and Samoa in the central South Pacific. But the Polynesians were content to stay put after that. They hardly moved from their new island homes for centuries.

With the onset of the Medieval Warm Period, though, Polynesian explorers again began paddling farther and farther out to sea.

The adventurers first established settlements in eastern Polynesia—the Cook, Society, and Marquesas islands. Hawaii was colonized later, perhaps around 1000.

Easter Island (now known as Rapa Nui)—far out in the Pacific Ocean, 1700 kilometers (1000 miles) from its nearest neighbor—was settled by Polynesians in 1200. And between 1250 and 1300, Polynesian canoeists landed on the shores of New Zealand. It was the last major land mass to be settled by humans.

At the time, the warm climate of New Zealand welcomed the Polynesians. They could grow the same foods as in their more tropical homeland, such as sweet potatoes. Higher sea levels, resulting from glaciers melting at the north and south poles, created ideal conditions for gathering crabs, clams, and fish in the shallows around New Zealand's coast.

But it didn't last. When the Medieval Warm Period gave way to a colder, less predictable climate in about 1300, the shift devastated many Polynesian settlements in the South Pacific.

New Zealand quickly returned to more extreme seasons. Winters were much colder, and sweet potatoes no longer grew. The shellfish that the settlers relied on became scarce as dropping sea levels left the shallows high and dry. The colonists abandoned their seaside life and moved inland, becoming hunters. They killed off the last of New Zealand's flightless moa birds at about this time and gathered fern roots and other wild plants that could survive in the changed climate.

GRAPE BRITAIN

According to historians, more than 50 wine-producing grape farms, or vineyards, were scattered across southern England during the Medieval Warm Period. Many believe English wine was unthinkable at any other time in the nation's history; temperatures were typically too cold for growing grapes.

Wine was important in medieval times. It was used in church ceremonies—and many of the early winemakers in England were Benedictine monks. The drink also preserved the vitamins and nutrients of grapes into winter.

When the Medieval Warm Period came to an end in about 1300, England virtually stopped making wine. Nowadays, as the climate warms once more, as many as 400 vineyards dot England's southern countryside.

In the centuries after the Medieval Warm Period, very few vineyards survived in chilly Britain. But since the 1950s, growing grapes for English wine has made a comeback.

THE EMPTY PUEBLOS

From inside her low, stone house in what is now the southwestern United States, the young girl watched the afternoon sun as its pink light slanted through the window. In the shadows nearby, her mother cooked paper-thin *piki* cornbread over the smoking coals of a fire. A decorated clay pot was warming nearby, but there was little stew in it. The year was 1150, and the girl and her mother were among the Anasazi people who lived and farmed in Chaco canyon located in present-day New Mexico

"We're not ready," the girl said sadly, "but the harvest time has come."

Only recently she had learned from her father the ancient art of marking the seasons by tracking the sun. She could see from where the sun was setting over the canyon boulders that it was time to bring in the corn. But after another season of little rain, this was not the welcome news it used to be. The fields were cracked and dry, and the crops were withered and small.

In the gloom of the gathering evening, the girl shuddered when she thought of the hunger and hardship in the season ahead.

In Europe, the Medieval Warm Period ushered in five centuries of relative comfort and stability. But the climate was far less kind to people in other parts of the world. For the ancient Anasazi civilization, it was a time of tragedy and collapse.

These Anasazi ruins in Chaco canyon were the largest structures built in North America until the first skyscraper went up in the 1880s.

READING THE TREES

The story of the Medieval Warm Period drought that brought the Anasazi civilization to its knees is told by the trees. Scientists uncovered clues to the four-century dry period by examining thin cylinders of wood bored out of the trunks of ancient trees.

Outside of the tropics (where trees grow year-round), trees have distinct rings that mark each growing season. The number of growth rings shows the age of the trees.

Each ring also provides a climate "signature." Seasons of strong growth leave thick rings, while seasons of stunted growth leave narrow ones. Other qualities, including how tightly packed the cells are and the form of carbon atoms, help researchers discover temperature and rainfall patterns.

Wood core samples from the United States and southern Canada show that the centuries between 900 and 1300—matching the Medieval Warm Period— were the driest in the past 1200 years.

Tree growth rings that show good growing seasons (wide rings) and poor ones (narrow rings) provide clues to past climates.

More than a thousand years ago, the Anasazi people (from the Navajo word for "ancient ones") built one of the earliest complex societies in North America. They lived among the stark desert canyons of the Colorado Plateau—one of the harshest landscapes on the continent.

The altitude of the plateau, high above sea level, meant unpredictable rains and extreme weather. In a single day, temperatures could fluctuate from freezing to warm, or from pleasant to scorching. Yet the Anasazi thrived there for almost 500 years.

Skilled farmers, the Anasazi took advantage of natural springs and rainwater to transform desert into cropland, cultivating corn, beans, and squash. Like the Mayans, they developed canal systems, dams, and reservoirs to channel and store the limited rain. They became skilled artists, traders, and creators of beautiful pottery.

Chaco canyon was the Anasazi capital. There, about a dozen enormous, multistory houses (*pueblos*, as the Spanish would call them later) were built from mud and wood—one of these, Pueblo Bonito, contained more than 650 rooms. The pueblos were home to Anasazi leaders and other wealthy citizens. They also served as government headquarters and a place for religious ceremonies.

Beginning in about 900, however, the American southwest was hit by what scientists call "an epic drought," a generally dry period almost 400 years long. The climate shift spelled disaster for the Anasazi. In about 1130, the plateau was wracked by a series of particularly dry spells—some lasting decades.

A scene like the imagined one above with the Anasazi girl and her mother may well have marked the beginning of the end. Remnants of pottery and cooking hearths found in the pueblos indicate that sometime between 1150 and 1200 the ancient ones of Chaco canyon called it quits. Anasazi communities in other canyons were abandoned when another drought struck in 1280 and lasted 26 years.

The Anasazi left their homes and historic civilization behind and scattered or moved to southern New Mexico. One community may have cleared out all at once—a carefully organized migration rather than a few families at a time. Under the skies of the Medieval Warm Period, the hopes of the Anasazi were drained dry by the sun.

THE LITTLE ICE AGE: WITCH WEATHER

CAULDRONS OF COLD

One late spring morning in the German town of Würzburg, Barbara Gobel woke to find the world gripped in a shocking, icy cold.

It was May 27, 1626. Barbara had been looking forward to summer. But there, in its place, was the cruel return of winter. Frozen rivers and lakes lay eerily still. Under a windless gray sky, rooftops and fields were white with frost.

Barbara's neighbors saw it, too. Staring from their windows and their doors, they gasped; not even the oldest great-grandmother had seen such a severe frost so late in the spring.

Beyond the farmhouses, field after field of grape shoots and many of the grape vines drooped, killed by the frost. The promising green blades of wheat and other crops were also destroyed. Hopes for a good harvest withered in the pale, icy shadows.

Barbara was a teenager, old enough to know that the crop-killing cold meant trouble. Many people would go hungry.

The strange Little Ice Age climate of medieval Europe led many people to suspect that evil forces were responsible.

Many would become desperate. But Barbara could not have guessed that the morning's terrible chill would also freeze to ice the hearts of her fellow townspeople.

The citizens of Würzburg weren't simply distressed by the abrupt change in the weather. They were frightened. How could such a terrible and unnatural thing happen? For the superstitious peasants, the answer seemed obvious: witchcraft.

In the months that followed, the authorities in Würzburg and other communities organized witch hunts, gathering up the most vulnerable suspects (mainly poor women or widows) and torturing them until they confessed.

Soon, officials claimed to have uncovered a sinister plot: the witches had planned to destroy all the grapes and wheat for several years until people became so hungry they would eat each other.

We can't know what Barbara Gobel thought of these stories before authorities arrived at her door. No records tell

COLD CLIMATE, COOL VIOLINS

Stradivarius violins are perhaps the most famous and valuable stringed instruments in the world. No one knows what makes them so musically perfect, but recently two researchers have proposed that the Little Ice Age might have had something to do with it.

Instrument-maker Antonio Stradivari set up his shop in northern Italy in 1680. There, he used spruce wood from the Italian Alps to make the all-important top of his violins—the "sound board" that vibrates to improve the tone.

In 2006, a Stradivarius violin, similar to the instrument pictured here, sold for $3.5 million. Several hundred violins made by Antonio Stradivari survive today.

Between 1645 and 1715, the Little Ice Age was at its coldest. This 70-year-long cold snap stunted the growth of mountain trees. Poor growth caused tight growth rings. The wood of spruce trees became dense and strong—perfect for improving the musical tone of violins.

The researchers say that the Stradivari recipe for the perfect violin has never been reproduced because the same prolonged cold conditions have not been repeated.

how Barbara reacted when she too was charged with being a witch.

The executioner's logbook tells us only that Barbara Gobel was just 19 when she was tied to a stake and burned to death. She was, says the logbook listing her death, "the fairest maid in Würzburg."

A CLIMATE OF FEAR

Young Barbara Gobel was one of 900 people killed for witchcraft in Würzburg in the years after 1626. Another 600 were burned in nearby Bamberg and 900 more in Mainz. Not far away, in Rhineland and Westphalia, about 2000 accused witches were put to death.

Religion contributed to deadly weather-related superstition in the 16th and 17th centuries. The Bible states, "Thou shalt not suffer a witch to live," and many innocent victims died as a result.

A SPOTLESS SUN

Just as the Medieval Warm Period was likely a time of many sunspots, the Little Ice Age began as the sun abruptly became less active. During one 70-year period from 1645 to 1715, sunspots were hardly visible at all. Those years were also the coldest of the Little Ice Age.

The period is known as the Maunder Minimum.

British astronomer Edward Maunder studied more than 200 years of astronomical records, reporting his discovery of this unusual pattern in the 1890s.

Fewer sunspots may have had only a slight effect on global cooling, but scientists say that less solar activity may have triggered changes to winds and ocean currents. That caused even colder temperatures in northern continents such as Europe and North America.

Witch hunts reached a climax in Europe between 1626 and 1630. About one million people are believed to have been burned, hanged, strangled, drowned, or beheaded for witchcraft between 1200 and 1900, and most of the executions took place during the 16th and 17th centuries. The practice even spread across the Atlantic Ocean to Salem, Massachusetts, in the 1690s.

The causes of this senseless and terrible violence have been debated for years. Some suspect that a superstitious church was behind it. (In the 1480s, Pope Innocent VIII announced that he believed weather-making witchcraft was real.) Others blame the fear that emerged after bubonic plague swept through Europe, killing millions during the 14th century.

Researchers now say that something else contributed to this bizarre period. The witch hunts of Europe took place during a time of climate upheaval known as the Little Ice Age.

Five hundred years of relatively mild weather known as the Medieval Warm Period ended abruptly around 1300. Average temperatures fell, and the Little Ice Age began.

The cold was hard enough—alpine snowcaps crept down mountains, shifting their snowy limits downhill by about 100 meters (over 300 feet)—but the Little Ice Age also brought wild, unpredictable weather. Sometimes storms raged and floods surged. Other times, the cold was deep and bitter.

This chilly, restless climate lasted for almost six centuries. And it coincided with some of the most harrowing times in the history of Europe, China, and elsewhere.

VANISHED VIKINGS

What happened to Greenland's Vikings? After all their adventuring in the North Atlantic, the Vikings who colonized Greenland in 980 completely disappeared from their settlements less than five centuries later.

Scientists have found clues to explain this mystery. Oxygen and hydrogen atoms exist in different forms that partly correspond to temperature. In a core of ice drilled from a Greenland glacier, these telltale atoms show a dramatic cooling in the middle of the 14th century—the beginning of the Little Ice Age.

The climate shift likely meant more sea ice around Greenland. Ship traffic to

In the beginning, the arrival of the Little Ice Age was regarded as fun.

In England, many Londoners were surprised and delighted to see the River Thames, which flows through the city, freeze solid during the winter of 1309. People cheerfully skated here and there, and, for the first time, ice festivals were held in the city. Vendors set up booths on the ice, and the river was transformed into a bustling fair.

But the fun didn't last. In about 1315, a constant rain began to fall on England and much of the rest of northern Europe.

With the onset of the Little Ice Age, Greenland became a land of snow and ice, and life grew unbearably harsh for the Viking settlers.

and from the settlements would have slowed and then stopped. Hunting and farming also became more difficult, and the colonists grew desperate.

Archeological digging at one Greenland farm revealed that the settlers became so hungry they ate all their livestock and, finally, the family hunting dog. A leg bone of the animal showed marks where a knife had carved its scrawny meat.

LONDON'S GREAT FIRE

The climate of the Little Ice Age was not only cooler; it often swung from one extreme to the other. Researchers say that the hot, dry summer of 1666 is an example of this climate seesaw—and one that changed the history of London forever.

Just past midnight on September 2, 1666, a fire broke out in London's Royal Bakery. The relentless heat of the summer had made the city's cheek-by-jowl wooden houses tinder dry.

For almost four days, the Great Fire of London raged out of control. It swept from one side of the city to the other, incinerating almost everything in its path. When the flames were finally put out, about 84 churches and 13,200 houses were rubble, leaving 100,000 people—one out of every six Londoners—without a home.

From May through August that year, Little Ice Age storms lashed the landscape. Fields turned into muddy ponds.

The next year was worse. In the endless rain, little could be planted and little would grow. According to one writer, the grain crop was the worst in almost 350 years. Wheat prices soared, and many people couldn't afford to buy bread. Meat became scarce after millions of sheep, goats, and cattle starved without hay or other feed.

From Britain to Poland, all across northern Europe, people found it harder and harder to feed themselves and their children. Hunger spread as the deadly partner of the wet cold.

Soon, dark and desperate figures began scrounging through fields and streets for anything to eat. Some said grave robbers were scooping out and eating the brains of bodies they uncovered. Others said starving people skulked in the shadows and snatched children as they walked by. These kidnappers were not interested in ransoms but killed the children to make a meal.

Historians still debate whether these tales of cannibalism are true, but there are many such stories from this time. The early years of the Little Ice Age left people so hungry they would do almost anything to survive.

This was the beginning of a period historians call the Great Famine. In about 1321, an unknown English poet chronicled the time in a verse called "Poem on the Evil Times of Edward II."

> When God saw that the world was so over proud,
> He sent a dearth on earth, and made it full hard.
> A bushel of wheat was at four shillings or more,
> Of which men might have had a quarter before ....
> And then they turned pale who had laughed so loud,
> And they became all docile who before were so proud.
> A man's heart might bleed for to hear the cry
> Of poor men who called out, "Alas! For hunger I die ...!"

No one knows how many died during this introduction to the Little Ice Age, but records suggest the toll was terrible. For instance, in the city of Ypres in what is now Belgium, the burial register says that 2794 of its citizens—a tenth of the city's population—were buried between May and October 1316. Some historians say that across large parts of northern Europe, one in every 10 people died of starvation or disease.

CHINA AND THE BLACK DEATH

China in the 14th century was ruled by Mongol kings. The Mongols of northern Asia, led by Kublai Khan, had conquered China half a century earlier. The influence of the Mongolian empire spread from southern China across Asia to the Black Sea.

Beginning in 1332, disaster struck when China was flooded by persistent torrential rains. Water surged down the great valleys of the Yellow and Yangtze rivers—among the longest waterways in the world. Entire villages and towns were swept away. As many as 7 million people died in what one writer called "one of the greatest weather disasters ever known."

But the floods were only the beginning of the tragedy. Researchers believe that the flooding—followed by years of drought—created the right conditions for the worst outbreak of bubonic plague known to history.

Bubonic plague is a strain of deadly bacteria that are mainly passed between fleas and their rat hosts. (Both the fleas and the rats eventually die from the disease.) The plague is naturally present in Asia, but it does not normally infect people. When rat populations crash abruptly, however, fleas can't find enough rats to feed on. In desperation, they bite humans, infecting them with the illness.

The weather disasters in China may have caused a massive rat die-off that left fleas searching for food—and finding humans. The post-disaster poverty likely also brought more people in contact with the remaining rats.

The plague took hold in China and spread quickly. By about 1346, an estimated 35 million people had died in that country. Then the killer crossed into Europe.

Many stories exist to explain the plague's arrival in Europe. In some versions, the disease traveled with caravans along an ancient trade route known as the Silk Road—a network of routes that allowed Europeans to trade for silk fabrics and other goods from China. In other accounts, Mongolian cattle herders carried the disease after they were forced by drought to leave their homelands in search of better pastures.

Mongolian forces were rumored to have spread the plague as they raced across the steppes of central Asia, sacking every town they came to. One Mongol army was stricken with the

Mongol warriors spread their empire's influence across almost a quarter of the Earth's land area. They may also have spread the plague.

disease even while it fought to take control of a Genoese port on the Black Sea. The town of Caffa (now known as Feodosiya, Ukraine) was an important trading gateway to Europe. The Mongols, so the story goes, decided to turn the tragedy to their advantage and began catapulting infected corpses into the town. The Genoese fled, but not before the deadly bacteria hitched a ride with them to Europe.

Between 1348 and 1350, the plague cut through European towns with the efficiency of a scythe, felling millions of people. Some say half the population on the continent dropped dead from the disease. Others say towns and cities throughout Europe lost between one-eighth and one-third of their population to the plague. Overall, between 20 and 50 million people are believed to have been killed.

The plague finally subsided in 1351 after devastating nearly all of Europe's most populated cities. It reappeared several times over the next 50 years, but the earliest outbreak was the most terrible. Hundreds of villages were entirely wiped out. The population of western Europe did not return to its pre-1348 level for 150 years.

THE LOST COLONY OF ROANOKE

In the often dreary Little Ice Age climate of 16th-century England, the paintings of John White must have been attractive to Londoners. The pictures had been painted in 1585, while White was on an expedition to North America. They showed the New World as a kind of paradise, complete with pineapples, basking crocodiles, and smiling natives.

England was anxious to settle colonies in the New World before its rival, Spain, acquired too much influence. White, with

CLIMATE'S ANGRY SEAS

Atlantic hurricanes, such as Isabel (pictured here in 2003), were fierce and frequent during the last half of the Little Ice Age.

The Little Ice Age was among the Atlantic Ocean's most wind-whipped and turbulent times. Scientists have re-created the history of hurricane strikes on an island in Puerto Rico over the past 5000 years by examining cores drilled from the bottom of an island lagoon. The cores show layers that have settled on the lagoon bottom.

Most show dark, rich mud—until a hurricane blasts in. The hurricane's high waves wash seawater over the reef, into the lagoon. Sand and seashells in the lagoon layers are evidence that a huge storm has struck.

Atlantic hurricanes were uncommon from about 1000 years ago until 300 years ago. But between 1700—the coldest period of the Little Ice Age—and 1850, 16 major hurricanes churned up the Atlantic seas. How seriously this stormy time affected sailing ships is unclear, but on the other side of the Atlantic, 42 vessels were sunk off the coast of Ireland in a single night and morning: January 6, 1839, is remembered in Irish stories as *Oiche na Gaoithe Moire*—the Night of the Big Wind.

Drought and poor harvests may have strained relations between Roanoke Island natives and the English settlers there between 1587 and 1590.

the help of his art, managed to persuade more than 100 people to return with him to create the first of these settlements.

They landed on Roanoke Island, off the shores of what is now North Carolina, on July 22, 1587. Among the settlers was White's own daughter, who, not long after their arrival, gave birth to Virginia Dare—the first English child born in North America.

A month later, White returned to England for supplies. The trip was to take three months. But England was fighting a sea war with Spain, and White's ship was ordered not to sail. He wasn't able to return to Roanoke Island until three years later. On August 17, 1590, he finally landed at the settlement, and what he found astonished him—the colony was gone.

THE BROKEN CONVEYOR

What triggered the onset of Europe's Little Ice Age? One theory suggests that a breakdown in the Atlantic Ocean's heat-delivery system may have been a factor.

The world's oceans work like an enormous conveyor belt. Water is warmed by the sun at the equator, then moved by currents to colder areas. In the North Atlantic, warm water that flows north along Europe's coast—called the Gulf Stream—helps to keep that continent from getting too frigid.

The conveyor is powered by water temperatures—and salt. Surface water cools as it flows north, and evaporation causes salt to concentrate in it. By the time it reaches the Arctic, the surface current is cold and heavy with salt, causing it to sink. Less salty, warmer water is pulled north to replace it. Deep down, the cold water is pushed south, where it will slowly rise as its salt content decreases again.

During the Medieval Warm Period, scientists theorize that fresh water melting from arctic glaciers may have diluted the water arriving in the north. No longer as salty, it didn't sink as much. The conveyor system stalled, and the ocean's heat-delivery service to Europe stopped cold.

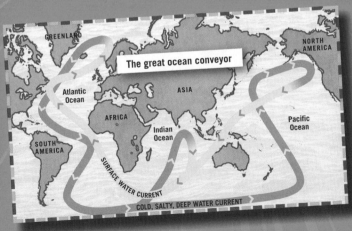

The great ocean conveyor

GREENLAND

NORTH AMERICA

Atlantic Ocean

ASIA

AFRICA

Indian Ocean

Pacific Ocean

SOUTH AMERICA

SURFACE WATER CURRENT

COLD, SALTY, DEEP WATER CURRENT

The mystery of the lost colony has puzzled historians for centuries. The only clue at the time was the word "CROATOAN" carved into a tree at the site. (Some accounts say it was carved into the fort gate.) The island of Croatoan was south of Roanoke, and its natives were known to be friendly.

White's efforts to reach Croatoan were dashed by storms, and he was forced to return to England. Many years passed before anyone visited the island, and no sign of the settlers was ever found.

Some researchers believe the colony members may have integrated with the Chesapeakes, a nearby native tribe. Or they may have been attacked by other natives and killed. Recently, scientists have uncovered evidence that the Little Ice Age's unstable climate may have had a hand in events.

Studying the growth rings of ancient trees, researchers found that the three years from 1587 to 1589 marked the driest three-year period in the region in the past 800 years. The entire southeastern United States was affected by a massive drought that was particularly severe in the area around Roanoke.

VOLCANOES: A CHILLING FURY

A BLAST OF DARKNESS

"Boom. Boom. Boom."

The thunderous noise rolled out of the distance and rattled Indonesia's tropical calm. It was evening, and the usual whir of jungle insects was startled into silence.

At Djokjakarta on the island of Java, garrison soldiers looked at one another and came to the same conclusion—cannons. A battle was raging not very far away. But who? Where?

The date was April 5, 1815. Four years had passed since the British had driven Napoleon Bonaparte's French soldiers out of Java. The angry noise of war was thought to be gone from the tropical islands, and the roar of distant guns took everyone by surprise.

Djokjakarta's commanders, thinking the next outpost to the south was under vicious attack, scrambled to send troops to help. They marched swiftly through the jungle, hoping to arrive in time to rescue their comrades.

"Boom. Boom."

A few hundred kilometers away, the captain of the *Benares* heard it, too. The ship quickly set sail from the island of Sulawesi. With Dutch troops aboard, the captain was determined to interrupt what he thought was an attack by pirates on one of the islands to the south.

For three days, the *Benares* searched without finding the cause of the commotion. The seas were peaceful, the islands unharmed. In Java, the troops also found nothing out of the ordinary.

What was going on? The colonial soldiers stationed in the South Sea islands scratched their heads. Five days passed. Then, at seven p.m. on April 10, 1815, the answer to the puzzle announced itself with a dramatic blast.

"Ka-BOOM."

Volcano! The 1815 eruption of Mount Tambora—a volcano that many had thought was extinct or not even a volcano at all—was the largest, deadliest, most violent volcanic eruption in

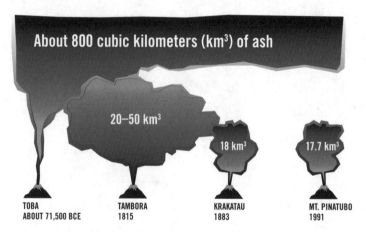

About 800 cubic kilometers (km³) of ash

20–50 km³   18 km³   17.7 km³

TOBA
ABOUT 71,500 BCE   TAMBORA
1815   KRAKATAU
1883   MT. PINATUBO
1991

Mount Tambora, far more explosive than any other volcano in the past few hundred years, is dwarfed by the prehistoric eruption of Toba. The amount of ash from each volcano is calculated as if it were compressed into measurable solid rock.

BRUSH WITH EXTINCTION

Bromo, a dormant volcano in Indonesia, has become a tourist attraction. But 71,000 years ago, another Indonesian volcano, Mount Toba, nearly wiped humans off the planet.

No eruption in the past 2 million years has matched the blast of Toba. The Indonesian volcano blew up around 71,000 years ago and changed the climate so much that it almost wiped humans off the planet. Our species, say researchers, was reduced to just a few thousand individuals—a number so small that disease or predators might have finished us off.

The Toba explosion was 40 times larger than the 1815 eruption of Tambora. Researchers say the ash and material sent skyward by the volcano would have been enough to block much sunlight from hitting Earth for several years.

The summers following the blast may have been as much as 15° Celsius (27° Fahrenheit) colder in the northern hemisphere.

A "volcanic winter" lasted for six years, followed by a thousand years more of cold, dry weather. Plant and animal life was devastated. Our species was no exception.

DNA studies of our genetic history show that humans faced a dramatic population crash around 70,000 years ago—the time after the Toba blast. Only people living in the warm, wet, tropical regions could have survived. From these small surviving groups, our ancestors later emerged to repopulate the planet.

recorded history. The April 5 explosions that had been mistaken for cannon fire were just a lead-up to the main event.

The enormous blast of April 10 blew off the top third of what many believe was the tallest mountain in Indonesia—almost as tall as the highest peak in the Rocky Mountains. It obliterated the villages at its feet on the Indonesian island of Sumbawa, killing more than 71,000 people there and on nearby islands.

Mount Tambora became a mountain of flames, and plumes of smoke and ash rocketed as high as 43 kilometers (27 miles) into the sky—about three times higher than most passenger planes fly. It was, by all accounts, spectacular.

A few hours later, a tsunami—a huge ocean wave triggered by the force of the explosion—hit villages on the shores of Java, hundreds of kilometers east. For days after the blast, the whole region was in complete darkness due to the amount of ash in the air.

These effects were felt far away, but Mount Tambora's influence extended farther still. Not because of the explosions or the tsunamis linked to the blast—because of climate change that reached around the globe.

VOLCANO WEATHER

"I well remember the 7th of June," wrote Connecticut clockmaker Chauncey Jerome, recalling the summer of 1816. "I was dressed throughout with thick woolen clothes and an overcoat on. My hands got so cold that I was obliged to lay down my tools and put on a pair of mittens."

Jerome had no way of knowing that, half a world away, Mount Tambora had blown itself to smithereens a year earlier. But scientists today have no doubt that the volcano blast was responsible for the summer deep freeze that amazed Jerome

BYRON'S "DARKNESS," SHELLEY'S FRANKENSTEIN

The cold and dreary summer that followed the explosion of Mount Tambora in 1815 proved to be a brooding inspiration for Lord Byron. The British poet and adventurer wrote his poem "Darkness" that summer while holed up in a cottage in Geneva, Switzerland.

> I had a dream, which was not all a dream.
> The bright sun was extinguish'd, and the stars
> Did wander darkling in the eternal space,
> Rayless, and pathless, and the icy earth
> Swung blind and blackening in the moonless air;
> Morn came and went—and came, and brought no day,
> And men forgot their passions in the dread
> Of this their desolation; and all hearts
> Were chill'd into a selfish prayer for light …

A visitor to Byron's cottage, Mary Shelley, is believed to have hatched the idea for her famous horror story, *Frankenstein,* at about the same time. The novel inspired by the gloomy season centers on humanity's meddling in the forces of nature.

Lord Byron was known for bouts of moodiness and melancholy—a poetic match for the dreary weather of 1816.

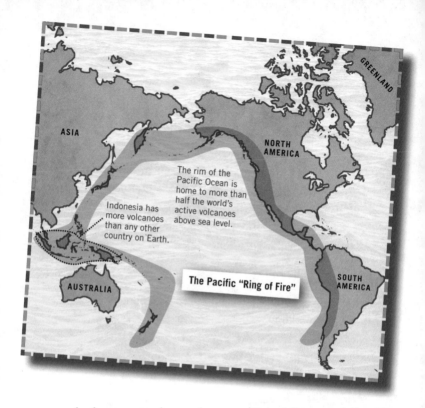

ASIA

GREENLAND

NORTH AMERICA

The rim of the Pacific Ocean is home to more than half the world's active volcanoes above sea level.

Indonesia has more volcanoes than any other country on Earth.

The Pacific "Ring of Fire"

AUSTRALIA

SOUTH AMERICA

and others across the northeastern United States and Canada, as well as Europe.

The climate around the world was abruptly knocked for a loop. The year 1816 came to be known as "the year without a summer," and its effects on life were dramatic.

Mount Tambora sent more ash into the sky than any other eruption in the previous 500 years. Scientists say the material included about 60 million tonnes (66 million tons) of sulfur gases. While volcanic dust and ash usually drift down within weeks or months, sulfur gases and other chemicals—called aerosols— that reach Earth's upper atmosphere can float there for years. They can affect the planet's climate by blocking, absorbing, or scattering sunlight.

Research indicates that 1816 was the second-coldest year in the past 600. It spelled disaster for farmers throughout Europe and North America.

In New England, ice covered the rain barrels several times through early summer, and the ground was crunchy with frost. In Quebec, June snows were deep enough to reach the axles of horse-drawn carriages. More frosts struck in early July and late August. Crops were destroyed, and people went hungry.

In Europe, the crisis was even worse. Persistent rain and cold killed the grain and potato crops in Britain and Ireland. Harvests in the rest of Europe were poor. Grain prices doubled, and researchers say the famine of 1816 to 1817—made worse by outbreaks of disease that flourished in the poor conditions—became the most deadly Europe had seen in more than a century.

Scientists say that major volcanic eruptions—such as the explosion of Mount Tambora—may have periodically knocked Earth's climate off kilter since the beginning of time. Volcanic gases carried by winds can cause cooling and other climate shifts that persist for years.

Evidence of long-ago volcanic eruptions can often be found as chemicals and ash trapped in the ice layers of ancient glaciers. Recent research into these clues suggests that human history has frequently been affected by these blasts of the past.

REMARKABLY UNSEASONABLE WEATHER

In 1258, the monk called Richer peered from his abbey window in the town of Sens in central France. The friar was startled to see that the dull fog and clouds remained settled over the countryside. They

The mighty volcano that blew up in 1258, shooting ash and gases into the atmosphere and disrupting Europe's climate, has never been identified. (The volcano pictured here erupted in Mexico in 1943.)

had first darkened the skies weeks before and were mysteriously refusing to leave.

"What, then, shall I say about the fruits of the earth that year," he wrote, "when the weather was so remarkably unseasonable that the warmth of the Sun was hardly able, even a little, to reach the earth, and the fruits of that year could barely attain maturity, if at all? For so great a thickness of clouds covered the sky throughout that whole summer that hardly anyone could tell whether it was summer or autumn."

Someplace on the planet in 1258—no one knows exactly where—a tropical volcano exploded with such force that it literally sent a shiver around the world. Scientists say sulfur and volcanic matter found in polar glaciers show that the blast was likely stronger than any other eruption in the past 2000 years. And it had a major impact on the climate.

By examining European weather records from the time— many kept by monks like Richer of Sens—researchers have

SUMMER CHILLS

By looking at the growth rings of trees up to 600 years old, from hundreds of places around the world, scientists have revealed summer chills that they believe correspond to volcano-related climate change. The coldest summer of the period was in 1601, a year after the eruption of a volcano known as Huaynaputina in Peru.

The summer of 1816, a year after Mount Tambora exploded in Indonesia, was the second coldest in the record. The summers of 1884 and 1912 also set cold records, following the eruptions of Indonesia's Krakatau, and Katmai in Alaska.

found that England, France, Italy, and other places reported a persistent fog and unusually cold and rainy skies throughout the summers of 1258 and 1259.

The result was crop failures and food shortages. Thousands of villagers and country people fled to London, seeking help.

A CLIMATE FOR ART

Some volcanoes are powerful enough to shake up Earth's climate, but could they affect the art world as well? Recently, scholars have linked the work of two great painters to climate changes triggered by the eruptions of Mount Tambora in 1815 and Krakatau in 1883.

J.M.W. Turner was a British landscape painter when Mount Tambora exploded. Bold crimsons and orange-yellows in his twilight skies show up only in pictures painted after the eruption—a time when England experienced spectacular sunsets caused by the play of sunlight through volcanic gases.

Researchers have also linked the Krakatau blast to the swirling red and orange sky in Edvard Munch's painting *The Scream*. The picture of an abstract figure screaming, hands raised to the side of his face, is famous for capturing the anxiety of the modern age. Although it was painted years after the eruption, letters written by the artist suggest that its inspiration came when Krakatau's gases were streaking the skies with lurid color, even as far north as Munch's home in Oslo, Norway.

Many died there of starvation. France and Italy were also hit by famine. In the Middle East, people in what is now Iraq, Syria, and southeastern Turkey suffered without enough food.

The cold, damp climate created the right conditions for disease. An epidemic of an easily transmitted illness that was known only as "the great pestilence of April 1259" caused many deaths in London, Paris, Italy, and Austria. The nature of the sickness isn't known, but its symptoms—lingering chills, weariness, and sometimes death—suggest it was a flu.

HUAYNAPUTINA

The February 16, 1600, eruption of Huaynaputina in Peru also rocked the planet's climate. That blast launched rocks, ash, and debris high into the sky for almost three weeks. Volcanic ash covered an area the size of Great Britain. In the city of Arequipa, 70 kilometers (42 miles) to the west, the weight of ash was so great that roofs caved in.

Almost no one outside of Peru had ever heard of the volcano hiding in the Andes Mountains. But the gases and material spewed into the sky by the eruption of Huaynaputina affected people around the globe. Ash and volcanic glass have been found trapped in ice at the south pole.

Many churches and buildings in Arequipa, Peru—known as the "White City"—are made from pale volcanic stone. The 1600 eruption of Huaynaputina, 70 kilometers (42 miles) away, covered Arequipa in a thick layer of ash.

Geologists who study active volcanoes help us understand how major eruptions can affect the climate.

In central Europe, the moon and sun appeared reddish and faint. In Iceland, the sun's light was too weak to throw shadows, and in China, the sun was only a dim, red ball.

"The month of June was very colde," reported one British chronicler in the summer of 1601. "Frosts every morning." Italy was also reported to be cloudy, with freezing temperatures right into July.

Researchers examining tree growth rings say that the northern half of the world was about 0.8° Celsius (1.4° Fahrenheit) colder than normal during that season—the coldest summer in 600 years. In Scandinavian countries, the summer was among the four most frigid in the past 1500 years. The cold hit western North America, too, and frosts devastated corn crops there.

A BLAST HEARD AROUND THE WORLD

On August 27, 1883, Captain W.J. Watson was nearing the end of a long voyage from Belfast. Steering his small cargo ship, the *Charles Bal*, through the straits and islands of Indonesia, the captain was looking forward to reaching Hong Kong and spending some time ashore. As he passed within 16 kilometers (10 miles) of the Indonesian volcano known as Krakatau—or Krakatoa to many Europeans at the time—Captain Watson was relieved that the journey had been uneventful. Then the tedium ended in a most alarming way.

"We noticed some agitation about the point of Krakatoa, clouds or something being propelled from the northeast point with great velocity," recalled the captain. "Chains of fire appeared to ascend and descend between [the volcano] and the sky, while on the [southwest] end there seemed to be a continuous roll of balls of white fire. The wind, though strong,

The ash from the 1991 explosion of Mount Pinatubo in the Philippines covered an area of about 125,000 square kilometers (50,000 square miles).

PINATUBO AND THE SEA

"I heard ladies down the street screaming and crying. I rushed outside and there it was. It looked like a nuclear bomb had gone up, a huge mushroom cloud over the volcano."

Victor Gomez is the owner of a restaurant just 16 kilometers (10 miles) away from Mount Pinatubo in the Philippines, and he was describing what he saw when the volcano blew its top in June 1991. Pinatubo, the largest volcanic eruption of the past century, forced 200,000 people to flee their homes and caused the deaths of more than 300.

But researchers now say there was a positive side— the volcano helped slow the effects of global warming.

Pinatubo sent huge amounts of sulfur and gases into the atmosphere, which blocked and scattered sunlight. The resulting lower temperatures cooled the world's oceans and reversed the sea-level rise caused by warming. Studies show the sea level dropped 6 millimeters (.25 inch) within a year of the eruption and rose only very slowly over the next decade. A similar effect was seen in the years following the explosion of Krakatau in 1883.

THE ISLAND AND VOLCANO OF KRAKATOA, STRAIT OF SUNDA, SUBMERGED DURING THE LATE ERUPTION.—[See Page 614.]

the University, and of other talented persons, in whose presence | sustained by an inward conviction that, sooner or later
the astonished nobility of Suabia raised its chin and miffed. | would come.

Headlines about Krakatau's blast in 1883 appeared in European and North American newspapers the next day.

was hot and choking, sulphurous, with a smell as of burning cinders, some of the pieces falling on us like iron cinders."

The eruption of Krakatau was massive. The series of explosions obliterated most of the small island that was home to the volcano. Captain Watson and his crew were closer to the event than any other survivors. The captain managed to steer to safety through darkness "so intense that we had to grope our way about the decks."

The jolt from the lava-and-rock-spewing volcano created giant tsunamis that rose higher than a five-story apartment building. The huge waves pounded the shores of nearby islands and smashed more than 160 towns and villages along Indonesia's coast. As many as 36,000 people were killed. Elsewhere on the islands, ash fell continuously for three days, covering crops and destroying jungles.

Today, researchers know that the eruption of Krakatau was considerably smaller than that of Mount Tambora, nearly 70 years earlier. But new undersea telegraph cables linking Asia and England ensured that the Krakatau event became far better known. Thanks to telegraph messages sent by reporters living near the disaster, British newspapers carried stories of the eruption the day after it happened.

As fast as news of the eruption spread, so did the volcano's effects on the climate. Tree ring data indicate that the year after the Krakatau explosion was one of the 13 coldest in the past six centuries. The scientific Royal Society of London collected observations of sky hazes, colored suns, and dramatic sunsets from around the world for three years following the blast.

EL NIÑO: THE CHILD'S TANTRUMS

THE LIVING DEAD OF MADRAS

William Digby wasn't yet 30 years old when he first stepped ashore in Madras City (now called Chennai) in colonial India. The year was 1877, and Britain had taken control of India from the British East India Company some two decades earlier.

Digby had traveled here, far from his boyhood home in Wisbech, England, to make his name as a newspaperman. He was in Madras to become the new editor at the *Madras Times*.

The young journalist was not new to newspapers or to the problems in South Asia. He had spent the previous six years working at the *Ceylon Observer* in what is now Sri Lanka. He knew firsthand how unfair life could be for people living in British-ruled colonies. But nothing could have prepared him for the horrifying sight that greeted his arrival in Madras.

The streets of the city were filled with living skeletons. Out of the dry dust and the low drift of coal smoke, they emerged like

Two decades after the 1877–78 famine,
colonial India saw millions more starve during
another El Niño drought that began in 1897.

ghouls out of a nightmare. Thousands of people wandered about with skin sagging over fleshless bones. They shuffled hopelessly in and out of the shadows. Starvation had reduced them to stick figures.

Digby stared in horror.

Some found shaded corners where they could die out of the sun. Mothers, eyes wild with desperation, approached strangers to sell their children for the price of a bit of food. Infants were left by the roadside to fend for themselves.

Wherever Digby went that year, he found signs of mass starvation. Travelers told him of even more terrible scenes in the countryside far from the city limits. Every place was parched, and crops refused to grow. Crows perched above bodies that lay along the highways.

Farmers fed their animals with the straw that made up the roofs of their houses. When more desperation set in, the animals themselves were eaten, leaving nothing to pull the plows for the next year's planting.

India had been hit by a catastrophic drought. In the summer of 1876, a year before Digby's arrival, the monsoon rains of summer delivered only a quarter of their usual rainfall. Farmers, who count on the seasonal downpours for as much as 80 percent of the year's rain, had almost no water for their crops.

The next year, 1877, even less rain fell. The farm fields dried and cracked under the hot sun, and grain and rice withered. Throughout much of southern and central India, people had no food.

By the time it was over in 1878, Digby estimated that 10.3 million people had died. They were killed by hunger or by cholera, a disease that preys upon the starving. In some of the hardest hit areas, populations fell by a quarter. It was, by some accounts, the worst mass famine ever recorded.

SHORT, SHARP SHAKE-UPS

At the time, Digby and others laid much of the blame for the disaster at the feet of India's British government for doing nothing while Indians perished.

The governor of the colony, Lord Lytton, appeared more interested in celebrating the

EL NIÑO'S UNRULY TEMPER

Some El Niños arrive with the suddenness and ferocity of a kid throwing a tantrum. But the name El Niño—literally "the young boy" in Spanish—doesn't refer to its childish temper. It's named after a warm current in the Pacific Ocean that arrives alongside Peru at Christmastime. Sailors call it *la corriente del Nino*, meaning "the Christ child's current."

An El Niño begins when the winds over the tropical eastern Pacific Ocean become weaker than usual. Meanwhile, the sea surface becomes warmer, and this warmth spreads across a wide area. The combination can cause huge shifts in temperature, winds, clouds, and humidity levels for the regional climate. This, in turn, can trigger climate changes throughout the world. El Niño is usually at its worst from December through March.

Scientists are only beginning to understand the complicated processes that cause El Niños and their ability to stir up weather trouble all over the planet.

proclamation of Queen Victoria as the "Empress of India" in 1877 than in offering relief to the desperate poor. Britain continued to ship grain from India for sale in England even while people in the colony starved.

But at the root of the catastrophe of 1877–78 was another culprit, far more powerful than the British Empire. An El Niño climate cycle—one of the most severe in 500 years—had knocked the entire continent's weather system off course.

El Niño cycles are responsible for extreme weather events, including floods, around the world.

El Niño is the shortest of the Earth's climate upheavals—it can last just weeks or up to a few years. Since the end of the Little Ice Age, though, it has been the most significant climate event to shake up human societies.

El Niños are regular, occurring every two to seven years. Although they're triggered by changes to sea temperatures, currents, and winds in the eastern Pacific, their effects don't stop there. El Niños have the power—thanks to interactions in our upper atmosphere and in our oceans—to reach right around the world. Scientists call these long-distance effects "teleconnections."

The drought of 1877–78 was among the first to alert scientists to this idea. Records kept by colonial officials allowed scientists to link India's plight with events elsewhere. Millions also died from droughts in China, and hundreds of thousands

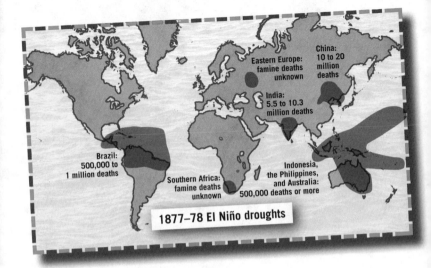

1877–78 El Niño droughts

Eastern Europe: famine deaths unknown

China: 10 to 20 million deaths

India: 5.5 to 10.3 million deaths

Brazil: 500,000 to 1 million deaths

Southern Africa: famine deaths unknown

Indonesia, the Philippines, and Australia: 500,000 deaths or more

perished during persistent dry weather in northeastern Brazil. Indonesia, Australia, and southern Africa all suffered without rain, yet Peru and San Francisco were extremely wet.

Teleconnections are what make El Niños so dangerous. Although some El Niños come and go with little effect on the climate, others are strong enough to cause deranged weather in many regions of the world. Lashing rains and terrible storms can cause floods and landslides in some places, while others are strangled with thirst and drought.

These disruptive climate cycles are not always easy to trace back through time. But researchers are uncovering clues to past El Niños—and there is growing evidence that El Niños and human calamity have often been companions.

MOCHE SACRIFICES GO UNREWARDED

In the dim light of the ceremonial pyramid called Huaca Cao Viejo in El Brujo, Peru, the Moche priest watched as the prisoners were led inside. Naked and bloody, with nooses around their

THE LITTLE GIRL

La Niña, or "the little girl," is the name for El Niño's flip side. Where El Niño is caused by weak ocean winds and a warmer sea surface, La Niña is linked to colder seas and stronger winds.

La Niña is not as common or as well known as El Niño, but it can still pack a punch. Often, its effects are the opposite—where El Niño brings drought, La Niña brings rain, for example.

La Niñas are responsible for wetter Asian areas near the western Pacific and for cool temperatures in northwestern North America. La Niña hurricanes over the Atlantic are twice as likely to hit the United States. A La Niña climate shift in 1998 brought the deadliest hurricane season in 200 years.

necks, the helpless captives seemed out of place in the ornate chamber. Colorful paintings decorated the ceiling and walls.

One by one, the prisoners were marched forward. The priest grabbed them by the hair and pulled their heads back. Ignoring their cries, he quickly cut their throats. A priestess stepped forward to catch the blood in a golden goblet so the priest could drink it.

These grisly ritual sacrifices were an important part of life for the Moche people of northern Peru. Two thousand years ago, the Moche built their civilization in one of the harshest, driest places on Earth. Regularly killing people to appease the gods must have seemed like a good way to tame the desert and lure the rains.

It seemed to them to work. The Moche civilization prospered for centuries—until a severe El Niño stepped in.

The Moche lived by farming and fishing for anchovies. Canals made with mud bricks channeled rainwater from the mountains, transforming the nearby desert into productive fields. Ruling warrior lords kept strict order. Religious ceremonies were held in the many large, mud-brick pyramids—such as Huaca

The Moche people were skilled artists and sculptors. The people of this complex culture were also good at managing their scarce water to tame the desert—for a time.

STORM STRIPES

Trying to discover past El Niños isn't easy. Stormy weather doesn't always leave a calling card. These days, however, scientists know where to look for clues.

In Ecuador, for instance, researchers drilled a column of mud from beneath a mountain lake. The layers that settled there, year after year, showed a pattern of dark and light stripes, like the stripes of a zebra.

The dark stripes matched years when normal rains carried dark mud and sand from surrounding slopes into the lake. The light stripes were layers of gravel,

Cao Viejo—painstakingly constructed along the coast.

Their society flourished. The Moche became skilled painters, sculptors, and metalworkers, crafting intricate gold jewelry inlaid with stones. Pottery, too, was exquisitely decorated, with designs featuring plants and animals or figures from Moche mythology.

Then, sometime around 560, the dark clouds of El Niño began to gather over the Pacific Ocean. Torrential rain broke through the mud-brick canal walls and filled streets and homes with water. Fields swelled with moisture until they became lakes. It was the beginning of almost 30 years of repeated flooding.

As crops failed, the Moche belief that human sacrifices would bring prosperity likely began to fail, too. The once-powerful priests and shaman-kings lost their authority. People starved, and society crumbled. Sometime around 750, the Moche civilization disappeared altogether.

which is only carried into the lake when water runoff is very powerful. And that only happens during major El Niño storms.

The researchers traced likely El Niño events back about 15,000 years and found that El Niño's current habit of showing up every two to seven years may only have started 5000 years ago. Before that, 15 years or more would pass between each El Niño. Scientists say the eastern Pacific may have been warmer at the time, making the sea temperature changes that trigger El Niños less likely.

Researchers have found clues to El Niño weather trapped in the ice layers of an Andean mountain ice cap. They report that the climate system that began in about 565 was a mega–El Niño. It was probably responsible for decades of wild, seesawing weather that tipped the delicate balance the Moche had struck with the desert around them.

A CLIMATE WITH REACH

By the end of the 18th century, citizens in the Mexican town of San Pedro Pareo and the residents of the former island of Jarácuaro were not on the best terms.

San Pedro Pareo and Jarácuaro are practically neighbors on Lake Pátzcuaro (a three-hour drive west of Mexico City). But in 1793 a dispute arose when each community claimed a piece of low, flat land as its own. The land, known as Pasteuras, connected the two municipalities so that people could walk between them. Although both places had been there for generations, they could be forgiven for not resolving the land dispute earlier—Pasteuras didn't exist before 1793.

Researchers say Pasteuras emerged from the lake only after the water level dropped by as much as a meter (over three feet) following years of intense drought. The island of Jarácuaro became a peninsula. Recent evidence indicates that the timing of this lake-level drop—and the squabble it caused—match the timing of a massive El Niño.

Scientists say the El Niño that occurred between 1789 and 1793 was among the most severe on record and had far worse consequences than a quarrel between neighbors.

Signs of that El Niño first appeared as a failure of monsoon rains in India in 1789. As many as 600,000 people died in

GUANO BUSINESS BOTTOMS OUT

Bird droppings are not usually the stuff of national pride. But for Peru in the 19th century, the feces of seabirds sparked a boom that helped define the nation and make it rich.

In the early 1840s, British and European businessmen visited Peru and smelled opportunity blowing ashore from tiny, rocky islets that were home to millions of seabirds. Over many years, these islands had become encrusted in piles of dried bird feces—known as guano. Some piles were higher than a 10-story building. And guano, full of nitrogen and phosphorus, makes terrific plant fertilizer.

An army of laborers began to shovel the stinking stuff onto ships bound for France, England, and the southern United States. Guano soon became Peru's largest export product.

Then El Niño struck. In 1861 and 1864, El Niño storms battered the seabird colonies, and the warm currents disturbed the fish that fed them. Birds died by the millions, and torrential rains washed away the guano piles. By the time another big El Niño hit in 1877–78, the guano boon had essentially ended, and Peru's economy was left reeling.

Seabirds, like this blue-footed booby, live on offshore islets in Peru, covering them with guano.

Madras in southeast India from the effects of drought. A year later, droughts were reported in Mexico, southern Africa, Indonesia, Australia, and a number of islands in the Atlantic, such as the Antilles.

At the same time, a lack of rain in the highlands of Ethiopia caused the Nile River to dwindle to very low levels. Farther south in Africa, droughts in Natal and Zululand resulted in severe famine. It caused a massive migration that dramatically changed how and where many south African tribes lived.

Researchers say a run-up to El Niño may also have caused the unusually cold winter of 1787–88 in western Europe. The deep freeze was followed by a late, wet spring and a disastrous summer drought that ruined crops across the region. Many say the crisis played a role in helping to spark the French Revolution of 1789.

EL NIÑO BECOMES A HOUSEHOLD NAME

The torrential rain of February 25, 1998, helped California set a record—the wettest February in more than a century. Two officers with the California Highway Patrol were sitting in their cruiser, amazed at the ferocity outside. The vicious storm was lashing trees, power lines, and houses.

Their radio crackled to life. The dispatcher said the officers were needed where Highway 166 was being threatened by the rising Cuyama River near Santa Barbara. The cops switched on their flashing lights and sped off through the gale.

The rain and fog reduced visibility to a few feet. The officers may not have seen the 90-meter (300-foot) gap where the river had already eaten away the highway. The cruiser likely swerved slightly before it tipped with a bump and pitched

In 1997–98, the most severe El Niño of the last century battered California, causing floods and landslides.

into the torrent. In a moment, it was gone, swept away by the churning brown river. The police officers didn't stand a chance.

El Niño's importance as a worldwide weather-maker has been known to scientists for a long time, but only recently has it achieved wider fame. In 1997 and 1998, the strongest El Niño in modern weather records made its effects felt around the world.

One of the hardest hit areas was California, ravaged by wild winds and rain. Soon, the name El Niño began to show up almost daily in newspapers and on television. Along the coast, water-soaked cliffs crumbled and houses fell into the sea as their owners fled. A 46-year-old man was killed when a landslide pushed a huge tree into his bedroom.

FALL OF A MODERN GOD-KING

El Niño's role in human history may include a bit part in the fall from power of Ethiopian emperor Haile Selassie. During much of his almost 45 years of power, the elegant and charismatic Selassie was celebrated as a hero in Africa and beyond. A religious movement in the Caribbean, Rastafari, even regarded him as a god-king.

But in 1972, when a major El Niño caused a severe drought in his country, Selassie faltered. The king was slow to recognize the crisis, and when he did, it was too late. His relief efforts didn't prevent more than 200,000 people dying of starvation and lack of water across northern Ethiopia.

To the Rastafari religious movement, former Ethiopian emperor Haile Selassie was the incarnation of God, whom they call Jah.

The famine continued through September 1974, and leaders in Ethiopia's army rebelled. They took over the government from the aging emperor and placed Selassie under arrest. Confined to his palace, Selassie died a year later under mysterious circumstances.

While El Niño storms raged in California, the Gulf Coast of Florida was battered, too. Mexico experienced unseasonably cold temperatures. Indonesia, afflicted by drought instead of rain, was so dry that the smoke of forest fires darkened the skies over the islands of Borneo and Sumatra.

In South America, Chileans enjoyed beach weather in the middle of their winter. In Africa, Kenya's rainfall was 100 centimeters (40 inches) above normal, and Somalia also suffered severe flooding. In Europe, a deluge of rain killed 55 people in Poland, and another 60 died because of flooding in the Czech Republic.

By the time it ended in June 1998, the ferocious El Niño that some scientists were calling "the climate event of the century" had left a worldwide trail of about $33 billion in damage and cost about 23,000 lives, mainly in Southeast Asia, Africa, and South America.

The consequences were not all bad. The 1997–98 El Niño may have been among the strongest and most destructive short-term climate upheavals we've ever seen, but it was also the most intensely studied. Observations of regional climate changes and El Niño's teleconnections with other climate disruptions around the world will help scientists better predict future events.

WAR: SKIES OF RAGE

GENERAL WINTER

How frustrating to face an enemy that could not be shot.

The thought must have occurred again and again to Sergeant Wolfgang Horn as he huddled against the night's bitter cold on December 4, 1941. He was just a day's march from Moscow, the capital city of the Soviet Union (now Russia), at the height of the Second World War.

The enemy that could not be fought was winter—"General Winter," the soldiers called it. Sergeant Horn and his fellow Germans sheltered themselves from the icy wind as best they could, ducking in and out of the blackened ruins of bombed-out houses.

It did little good. The temperature had fallen quickly after days of heavy snow. Thermometers showed –42° Celsius (–44° Fahrenheit). That's colder than the north pole usually gets in winter.

Hitler's invasion of the Soviet Union, 1941

"Our socks freeze and stick to our boots," Sergeant Horn wrote in his diary.

Turning up the collar of his thin overcoat, the sergeant shivered uncontrollably. The Germans had invaded the Soviet Union in summer and expected a quick victory. They now had little clothing or supplies after failing to take Moscow before winter set in.

When they could, the soldiers took clothes and boots from fallen Soviets, piling on layer after layer of lice-infested shirts and sweaters. Still hopelessly chilled, they huddled beside small fires or cupped frostbitten hands around the glowing ends of cigarettes.

In just two years, Nazi Germany had conquered much of Europe. Poland, Norway, Denmark, the Netherlands, Yugoslavia, Greece, and France had all fallen to the armies of Adolf Hitler. Moscow was to be a crowning achievement in Hitler's lightning invasion of the Soviet Union. Climate change helped to foil his plans.

Germany's invasion of the Soviet Union saw early success in 1941, but was frozen in its tracks by severe winters linked to El Niño cycles.

In the bitter dawn of December 5, 1941, Sergeant Horn and the other troops with Army Group Center woke from a short and chilly sleep. They started their camp stoves and warmed themselves as well as they could with watery coffee. A few did not wake up; they had frozen to death in their sleep. One regiment that had marched through the night suffered 300 cases of frostbite.

The Germans tried to start their tanks and trucks, but the big machines choked and stalled. They didn't have enough antifreeze. The lubricants to keep parts moving had become too thick in the arctic temperatures.

Then the quiet of the frigid morning was shattered by the menacing howl of Katyusha rockets—the Soviet Red Army was attacking first.

As Soviet troops poured across the ice-covered river and rushed at the German line, Sergeant Horn and his comrades scrambled for their guns. But many of the weapons wouldn't shoot. They were frozen in the cold.

The Soviet forces were better prepared. For weeks, new troops and supplies had been arriving at the battlefront, brought by trains insulated against the cold. The Soviet tanks were equipped with antifreeze, and the soldiers carried weapons lubricated to fire in the iciest conditions.

The Red Army and the cold were too much for the Germans. Over the sound of gunfire and rockets, Sergeant Horn heard the order from his commander: Retreat.

WEATHER AS A WEAPON

The Battle for Moscow is considered by many to have been a turning point of the Second World War. For the first time in that terrible conflict, the Germans were stopped. Despite 3 million German troops

A harsh El Niño winter may also have helped foil Napoleon Bonaparte's attempt to conquer Russia in 1812.

and thousands of tanks and airplanes, the invasion of the Soviet Union failed.

The Red Army claimed victory. But scientists say that a shift in climate also deserved credit, for seeming to fight on the side of the Soviet Union.

Researchers say the winter that helped repel the German attack on Moscow in 1941 was no ordinary one. The unusual cold was likely caused by a major El Niño in the eastern Pacific. Scientists believe the El Niño set off climate changes in many parts of the world, including Europe.

This El Niño began in the fall of 1939 and gathered strength through 1940 and 1941. By the time Hitler's army reached the outskirts of Moscow, the Soviet Union was beset by strange and unstable weather. Frigid temperatures and blizzards were interrupted by frozen rain and sleet.

The Battle for Moscow was not the first time climate change has been on the scene during a pivotal moment in military history. Nor would it be the last.

Although many historians hesitate to consider anything other than politics, social factors, and the personalities of leaders when looking at past wars, recent research is drawing more attention to climate shifts during times of conflict. Extreme weather has accompanied a number of significant battlefield victories and defeats.

BLOWN AWAY

In September 1588, the North Atlantic was white with foam. A huge storm tossed mighty Spanish warships around like bobbing corks on monstrous waves. The gale blasted the sailors with near-hurricane-force winds until they had to clutch at the rigging for fear of being swept into the sea.

The Spanish Armada of 1588 was a formidable fleet before it
was beaten by the British and smashed by Little Ice Age storms.

"There sprang up so great a storm on our beam," wrote
one captain, "with a sea up to the heavens so that the cables
could not hold, nor the sails serve us and we were driven ashore
with all three ships upon a beach covered with fine sand, shut
in one side and the other by great rocks."

The ships belonged to the Great Spanish Armada, a vast
fleet of 130 warships and merchant vessels all rigged for battle.
It was the largest naval fleet of its time, and it had sailed
to England to strike a decisive blow during the conflict of
1585–1604.

But the Great Armada sailed into the middle of 500 years
of tumultuous climate change—a period of harsh, cold, often
stormy weather that we now call the Little Ice Age.

CAN CLIMATE CHANGE LEAD TO WAR...

Politics, religion, and greed usually top the list of reasons for past wars. More people today, though, wonder if climate change should be on that list too.

Recently, scientists compared a 500-year history of armed conflicts around the world against the same period's history of warming and cooling. Tree growth rings, glacier ice cores, growth patterns in coral reefs, and weather records all offered clues.

The researchers looked at over 2900 wars fought around the world between 1400 and 1900 (during the Little Ice Age). They found two periods of intense warfare and violence from about 1450 to 1710 and from 1810 to 1860, separated by three periods of relative peace. These phases closely matched temperature shifts: colder centuries experienced almost twice as many wars as did the relatively mild 18th century. In China, the researchers found a similar relationship between temperature and warfare over a longer period between 1000 and 1911.

The link between war and weather is not a new idea. Many have speculated that climate upheavals can trigger famine, competition, and desperation that lead to fighting. This study, though, is the first to uncover a scientific connection between shifts in climate and the taking up of arms around the world.

Conflicts fought by Chinese soldiers flared up more often during cool periods with poor harvests between 1000 and 1911.

...OR CAN WAR LEAD TO CLIMATE CHANGE?

When Iraq's invading army was driven out of Kuwait during the Persian Gulf War of 1991, the Iraqis set the country's oilfields ablaze before they fled. More than 600 oil wells became spewing infernos. About 3.1 million barrels of oil burned every day, pouring thick, greasy smoke high into the darkening sky.

The smoke from these enormous fires blocked out the sun and actually caused the region to become cooler. But it could have been worse. Many prominent scientists worried that the smoke could affect the monsoons over India and Asia and perhaps cause a killer drought.

Fortunately, that didn't happen. But the episode was a reminder that modern warfare has the power to cause global climate change. Researchers studying the likely effects of a small, regional-scale nuclear war say that climate change caused by nuclear bombs blasting gas and material into the upper atmosphere would be even more deadly in the long run than the explosions or radioactive fallout.

Soldiers may be unaware of the climate effects of warfare, but scientists now think that changes to the atmosphere from bomb blasts and fires may affect us even after the fighting is over.

The Spanish fleet made it to the North Sea off England's east coast before being surprised by an attack by English ships. A planned land invasion was called off, and the Great Armada tried to escape back to Spain by rounding the north end of the British Isles and sailing south. And that's when the Little Ice Age decided to enter the war.

After surviving a fierce gale near the eastern side of Scotland in August, the fleet was hit by another storm as it sailed south. The ships leading the Armada rode the wild winds off the west coast of France. Those behind were caught in the seas near western Ireland. Many of these vessels were battered by furious winds until they smashed against the rocky coast.

Twenty-four Spanish ships were wrecked off the coast of Ireland. The Great Armada, which was expected to strike dread into the hearts of its enemies, lost more ships to the weather than to any battles with the English.

Researchers who have studied weather records kept by Armada captains say the fleet was caught by a kind of storm machine over the North Atlantic. This "squall factory" was the result of a change in the ocean's air-pressure system, linked to a Little Ice Age cooling of the sea surface. The North Atlantic saw the most intense storms of modern history during this period.

FALLING REIGN

The torrential rain outside the windows of Paris city hall must have struck Maximilien Robespierre as a bizarre twist of fate.

It was evening on July 17, 1794. Robespierre, who had risen to power as a leading figure in the French Revolution, planned to rally his supporters gathered in the square. He expected popular support would save him from his enemies in the new government.

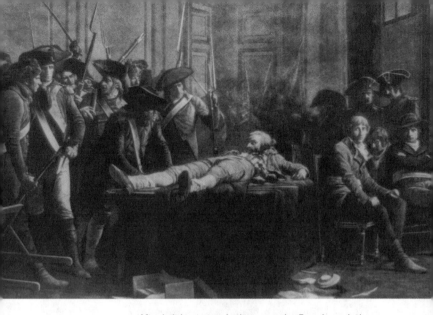

After helping to topple the monarchy, French revolutionary leader Maximilien Robespierre was interrogated and then executed by political rivals in 1794.

But a fierce summer storm swept over Paris. Just before Robespierre was to address the crowd below, a downpour sent people running for shelter. By the time Robespierre appeared at the window to speak, everyone had vanished. Only rainwater covered the dark cobblestone square.

Within hours, Robespierre was arrested by rival forces in the French National Assembly. A day later, he was executed by guillotine.

Ironically, a sudden change in the weather had sealed the fate of the revolutionary leader. Just six years earlier, climate change had helped spark Robespierre's beloved revolution.

For centuries, France, like most other nations in Europe, was ruled by a succession of kings and queens. In the late 18th century, King Louis XVI was on the French throne, and he and his courtiers enjoyed lives of outrageous extravagance.

GLOBAL WARMING AND DARFUR

In 2003, a civil war erupted in the Darfur region of Sudan, Africa. It became one of the bloodiest in recent history. The conflict—which has claimed as many as 200,000 lives—involves Arab nomads, African farmers, and rebels, but many now believe that climate may also have a role in the tragedy.

Since the early 1980s, rainfall in southern Sudan has fallen by 40 percent. Scientists say this drop—and the resulting drought—is likely linked to a rise in the temperature of the Indian Ocean caused by global warming.

Before the drought began, African farmers welcomed the Arab herders and let them graze their camels and share the wells. The friendliness ended when the rains stopped. Farmers fenced their land to protect their scarce water and pastureland. Fighting broke out and soon escalated into war.

Life is desolate for refugees from the war in Darfur—a war that arose "at least in part from climate change," says United Nations Secretary General Ban Ki Moon.

The beheading of King Louis XVI in 1793 meant the end of the traditional monarchy in France.

His residence in the Palace of Versailles was a display of opulence, with 1400 fountains, a Grand Canal 1.6 kilometers (1 mile) long, and a vast hall of mirrors. A magnificent opera hall was illuminated by 3000 beeswax candles for each performance.

In sharp contrast, more than three-quarters of the French were peasants, and many were desperately poor. Nearly all lived and worked on land owned by feudal lords who charged them heavy taxes.

The Little Ice Age was making life even harder for the poor. Severe winters through the mid-1700s had caused crop failures, and many peasants starved. The winter of 1787–88, however, was the worst. It was unusually frigid, possibly because of climate disruptions leading up to a massive El Niño.

The El Niño of 1789 to 1793 clobbered many regions of the world, including Europe. The harsh winter of 1787–88, followed by a late, wet spring and a summer drought, was a dramatic prelude.

People weakened by the cold were struck down by diseases and hunger. Crops failed and food prices soared. The peasants clamored for bread, and before long they were rioting in the streets. The first sparks of protest soon lit the fire of revolution.

As another frigid winter was followed by floods and drought, France continued to simmer with tension. An attempt by King Louis XVI to raise property taxes spurred angry opposition. Robespierre—a commoner and lawyer from northern France—was among the elected leaders of this group. He became popular for his attacks on the monarchy and his calls to make France more democratic.

Fearing that royal soldiers were about to prevent members of the National Assembly, including Robespierre, from meeting to push for change, mobs of people took to the streets in a melee of rioting and looting. In July 1789, crowds stormed the Bastille prison—a symbol of royal tyranny—and executed the prison governor. By August, the feudal system was abolished and the government transformed. The power of King Louis XVI was fading fast. By 1792, the king was removed from his throne and locked in prison.

"I vote for death," argued Robespierre during the king's trial. Louis XVI was beheaded on January 21, 1793. Robespierre's own death sentence came the following year. The winds of change continued to blow through France for decades to come—winds that many believe were strengthened by El Niño.

WEATHERING THE FUTURE

For Saad, a farmer, the Egypt of today isn't so different from the Egypt of ancient times.

Saad grows food on the flat, fan-shaped piece of land where the Nile River empties into the Mediterranean Sea. It is the same fertile area—known as the Nile delta—where Egyptians have grown crops for more than 5000 years. Although the delta is just a tiny fraction of Egypt's total land, almost half the nation's crops, including wheat, rice, and bananas, are farmed there. And 30 million of the country's 80 million people live in the region.

Saad's fields are near Rosetta, a three-and-a-half-hour drive northwest of the Egyptian capital, Cairo. These days, his farm chores include building dikes and digging channels. They may seem like odd jobs for a farmer, but Saad has to try to keep the rising water of the Mediterranean Sea out of his fields. The salt water would kill his plants.

Even with his dikes and ditches, Saad says he has to flush his fields regularly with fresh Nile water to wash the soil free

Salt water from the rising Mediterranean Sea threatens to ruin the Egyptian farm fields of the low-lying Nile delta.

of salt. Other farmers share Saad's problem, and it's getting worse.

It's another reason why the Egypt of today is like the Egypt of thousands of years ago—climate change is once again threatening this society.

Scientists say that sea levels—including the level of the Mediterranean—will rise between 30 centimeters and 1 meter (from 1 foot to over 3 feet) by the end of the century. Thanks to global warming, melting glaciers are pouring water into the world's oceans and seas at the same time that higher temperatures are causing them to expand.

A rise of one meter will flood a quarter of the Nile delta, forcing more than one-tenth of Egyptians from their homes. Around the world, about 100 million people living in low-lying

CLIMATE AND CREATURES

Like many animals around the world, the small European bird known as the great tit is threatened by today's fast-changing climate. The birds normally breed during the peak season for caterpillars. This ensures that they have enough food for their young. But their timing has been thrown off by warm springs that cause the caterpillars to hatch early.

Evolution, say scientists, may already be at work. The birds that survive will have what it takes—flexibility.

Researchers have found that those birds best able to adjust their egg-laying dates to match the peak caterpillar season are successfully raising more young. This ability to be flexible is coded in their genes, and they pass it on to their chicks. That means the more flexible population of great tits is pulling ahead.

Scientists have seen similar genetic changes in response to climate shifts by another bird called the European blackcap, by Canadian red squirrels, and by fruit flies. Although many predict global warming will wipe out millions of species, other populations may evolve the ability to go with the flow in an uncertain climate.

Climate change is affecting life for millions of plant and animal species, including these European great tits.

areas near the coast face the same prospect. A sea-level rise of 4 to 6 meters (13 to 20 feet) could follow in the coming centuries, leaving south Florida, much of Bangladesh, New Orleans, and many other seaside cities awash.

The disaster would be no less severe inland. Some 250 million Africans will likely find themselves without enough water. Tropical forests in some parts of the world will turn into grasslands. Great coral reefs will die back as oceans warm up. One group of scientists predicts that within the next decades, the American southwest will become as dry as it was during the Dust Bowl drought of the 1930s—but it will stay that way as far into the future as we can see.

ONE BIG GREENHOUSE

Saad's Egypt has gone through climate chaos before—a naturally occurring drought rocked the world of the pharaohs about 4200 years ago. But the crisis today is different. Global warming is happening faster and more dramatically than any other climate change seen by human civilization. And for the first time, it's our fault.

Our species has come a long way. From brainy apes, we've emerged to become builders of sophisticated cities, powerful computers, and pay-per-view satellite movies—but to do it, we've changed the atmosphere and our climate.

We dump carbon dioxide into the air every time we start an engine, light up an office, blast off a space shuttle, warm our homes, or turn on the TV. Carbon dioxide is created when we burn oil and other fuels to make power or heat. It's a "greenhouse gas." That means that, high in the atmosphere, it acts like the glass panes of a greenhouse, letting sunlight through and trapping heat inside.

Even just watching TV contributes to global warming. Electricity generation often involves burning coal, oil, or gas and releasing carbon dioxide.

Since about 1800, the time of the earliest steam engines and factories, we've increased the amount of carbon dioxide in the atmosphere by almost a third. That's upsetting the balance of atmospheric gases that once kept temperatures in check.

The changes we're seeing now are the price of our progress. Nature—the orbit and tilt of the Earth, the brightness of the sun, volcanic eruptions, sea currents, winds, and many other forces—has thrown plenty of climate curveballs in our past. But now we're throwing one of our own—and it's a doozy.

The worst effects of this new climate change may hit areas many of us have never heard of, but no place is immune. In 2003, a heat wave killed about 30,000 people across Europe. Two years later, Hurricane Katrina—one of the many big storms that are brewed by warmer oceans—caused 1500

Cycling instead of driving can help to reduce carbon emissions. Cars produce many times their weight in greenhouse gases every year.

CHANGING TO STOP CHANGE

Climate change can seem unstoppable, but each of us has the power to make a difference. The key to slowing global warming is cutting greenhouse gases. Unfortunately, we scarcely notice the things we do that release these gases because they're just part of our everyday lives. The first step is to become more aware. The second is to make some changes—and many are quite simple.

Using less hot water, for instance, is helpful. A third of carbon dioxide emissions comes from household power use, and a third of most home power bills is spent on heating water—for showers, dishwashers, and washing machines.

Driving less cuts the greenhouse gases released by cars. We can walk or ride a bike or a bus—a bus full of people means less carbon dioxide per person. We can turn off lights when we leave a room, shut down computers overnight, and set the thermostat a couple of degrees lower, or use an air conditioner only when it's very hot.

And, most importantly, we can keep learning. The more we know, the more we can do.

deaths after it smashed through sea walls and flooded New Orleans. The summer and autumn of 2007 saw hot, dry spells in Greece and in California that created the right conditions for huge wildfires to get out of control, scorching vast areas of forestland as well as hundreds of homes.

If we want to keep weather events from getting worse, we have to get serious about controlling greenhouse gases. Some leading scientists suggest that we need a 50 to 80 percent cut in greenhouse gas emissions by the time most of today's kids reach their 40s. That's just to keep the planet's temperature from becoming warmer than it's been in more than a million years.

THE DIRECTION OF HOPE

When climate change struck northern Africa and western Asia in 2200 BCE, a drought that lasted centuries hammered civilizations from the Akkad Empire of Mesopotamia to the Harappan in the Indus Valley. Ancient Egypt was devastated too—for a while.

Akkad and other societies collapsed entirely during the upheaval. Egypt, on the other hand, struggled through a period of famine, lawlessness, and tribal fighting, but it recovered and carried on for another 2000 years.

Egypt's solution to the climate crisis was straightforward— waterworks. When the droughts began, a few scattered communities began digging networks of canals to bring water from the shrinking Nile to the dry fields. The idea caught on, and a new dynasty arose.

The changing climate that threatens Egypt and other countries around the world today is far larger in scale than the calamity of ancient times, but there are similarities. The answer back

Solar panels generate energy and reduce our dependence on burning fuel.

then began with local people; the answer now must start with each one of us. By making wiser choices, we can help cut the greenhouse gases sent into the atmosphere.

The lucky part is that limiting these gases is entirely possible, and we have the freedom to choose how we live. We simply need to know where to start. The ingenuity and flexibility that served the Egyptians of ancient times should give us reason to be hopeful. Knowing the lessons human societies have learned about climate upheavals in the past may give us some ideas about planning for our own fast-changing and uncertain future.

FURTHER READING

Adams, Simon, and Katherine Baxter. *The Kingfisher Atlas of the Ancient World*. New York: Kingfisher Publishing, 2006.

Allaby, Michael, and Richard Garratt. *A Change in the Weather*. Facts on File Dangerous Weather Series. New York: Facts on File, 2004.

Arnold, Caroline. *El Niño: Stormy Weather for People and Wildlife*. New York: Clarion Books, 2007.

Barr, Gary. *Climate Change: Is the Earth in Danger?* Chicago: Heinemann, 2006.

DeMarco, Neil. *Second World War*. Hodder 20th Century History. London: Hodder and Stoughton, 2004.

Desonie, Dana. *Climate*. Our Fragile Planet. New York: Chelsea House, 2007.

DK Publishing. *Early Humans*. DK Eyewitness Books. New York: DK Books, 2005.

Evans, Kate. *Weird Weather: Everything You Didn't Want to Know About Climate Change But Probably Should Find Out*. Toronto: Groundwood Books, 2007.

Facklam, Margery. *Changes in the Wind: Earth's Shifting Climate*. San Diego: Harcourt Children's Books, 1986.

Fradin, Dennis, and Judith Fradin. *Witness to Disaster: Volcanoes*. Washington, DC: National Geographic Children's Books, 2007.

Furgang, Kathy. *Tambora: A Killer Volcano from Indonesia*. Volcanoes of the World. New York: PowerKids Press, 2001.

Gore, Al. *An Inconvenient Truth: The Crisis of Global Warming*. New York: Viking, 2007.

Hawkes, Nigel. *Climate Crisis*. Markham, ON: Fitzhenry and Whiteside, 2004.

Hynson, Colin. *Elizabeth I and the Spanish Armada*. Stories from History. Grand Rapids, MI: School Specialty Publishing, 2006.

Johnson, Kirk, and Mary Ann Bonnell. *Gas Trees and Car Turds: Kids' Guide to the Roots of Climate Change*. Golden, CO: Fulcrum Publishing, 2007.

Lourie, Peter. *The Lost World of the Anasazi: Exploring the Mysteries of Chaco Canyon*. Honesdale, PA: Boyds Mills Press, 2003.

Mattern, Joanne. *Leif Eriksson: Viking Explorer*. Explorers! Berkeley Heights, NJ: Enslow Publishers, 2004.

Miller, Lee. *Roanoke: The Mystery of the Lost Colony*. New York: Scholastic, 2007.

Morgan, Sally, and Jenny Vaughan. *Climate Change*. Earth SOS. London: Franklin Watts, 2007.

Perl, Lila. *The Ancient Maya*. People of the Ancient World. London: Franklin Watts, 2005.

Peters, Stephanie True. *The Black Death*. Epidemic! New York: Benchmark Books, 2004.

Seibert, Patricia. *Discovering El Niño: How Fable and Fact Together Help Explain the Weather*. Markham, ON: Fitzhenry and Whiteside, 2004.

Sloan, Christopher. *The Human Story: Our Evolution from Prehistoric Ancestors to Today*. Washington, DC: National Geographic Children's Books, 2004.

Spilsbury, Louise A. *Changing Climate: Living with the Weather*. Eustis, FL: Raintree, 2006.

Stein, Paul. *Droughts of the Future*. New York: Rosen Publishing, 2001.

Tanaka, Shelley. *Climate Change*. Toronto: Groundwood Books, 2006.

Tyldesley, Joyce. *Egypt*. Insiders. New York: Simon and Schuster Children's Publishing, 2007.

Unwin, Mike. *Climate Change*. Chicago: Heinemann, 2006.

Woodward, John. *Climate Change*. DK Eyewitness Books. New York: DK Books, 2008.

SELECTED BIBLIOGRAPHY

Today's Forecast

Kerr, R.A. "Global Warming Is Changing the World." *Science* 316 (2007): 188–90.

Kolbert, E. *Field Notes from a Catastrophe*. London: Bloomsbury Publishing, 2006.

Lamb, H.H. *Climate, History and the Modern World*. 2nd ed. Oxford: Routledge, 1995.

Ryan, W., and W. Pitman. *Noah's Flood: The New Scientific Discoveries about the Event that Changed History*. New York: Simon and Schuster, 1999.

Thuiller, W. "Biodiversity: Climate Change and the Ecologist." *Nature* 448 (2007): 550–52.

Beginnings: Mother Ice

Begun, D.R. "Planet of the Apes." *Scientific American* 289 (2003): 74–83.

Bobe, R., A.K. Behrensmeyer, and R.E. Chapman. "Faunal Change, Environmental Variability and Late Pliocene Hominin Evolution." *Journal of Human Evolution* 42 (2002): 475–97.

Fagan, B. *The Long Summer: How Climate Changed Civilization*. New York: Basic Books, 2004.

Lieberman, D.E. "Homing in on Early Homo." *Nature* 441 (2007): 291–92.

Linden, E. *The Winds of Change: Climate, Weather, and the Destruction of Civilizations*. New York: Simon and Schuster, 2006.

O'Brien, E.M. "What Was the Acheulean Hand Ax?" *Natural History,* July 1984: 20–23.

Drought: The Curse of Akkad

Abate, T. "Climate and the Collapse of Civilizations." *Bioscience* 44 (1994): 516–19.

Binford, M.W., A.L. Kolata, M. Brenner, J.W. Janusek, M.T. Seddon, M. Abbott, and J.H. Curtis. "Climate Variation and the Rise and Fall of an Andean Civilization." *Quaternary Research* 47 (1997): 235–48.

deMenocal, P.B. "Cultural Responses to Climate Change during the Late Holocene." *Science* 292 (2001): 667–73.

Diamond, J. *Collapse: How Societies Choose to Fail or Succeed.* London: Penguin Books, 2005.

Peterson, L.C., and G.H. Haug. "Climate and the Collapse of Maya Civilization: A Series of Multi-Year Droughts Helped to Doom an Ancient Culture." *American Scientist* 93 (2005): 322–30.

Weiss, H. "Desert Storm." *The Sciences,* May/June 1996: 30–36.

The Medieval Warm Period: An Adventurous Wind
Fitzhugh, W.W., and E.I. Ward, eds. *Vikings: The North Atlantic Saga.* Washington: Smithsonian Institution Press, 2000.

McGovern, T.H. "The Archaeology of the Norse North Atlantic." *Annual Review of Anthropology* 19 (1990): 331–51.

Muro, M. "New Site Suggests Anasazi Exodus." *Science* 290 (2000): 914–15.

Nunn, P.D., R. Hunter-Anderson, M.T. Carson, F. Thomas, S. Ulm, and M.J. Rowland. "Times of Plenty, Times of Less: Last-Millennium Societal Disruption in the Pacific Basin." *Human Ecology* 35 (2007): 385–401.

Zhang D. "Evidence for the Existence of the Medieval Warm Period in China." *Climatic Change* 26 (1994): 289–97.

The Little Ice Age: Witch Weather
Behringer, W. "Climatic Change and Witch-Hunting: The Impact of the Little Ice Age on Mentalities." *Climatic Change* 43 (1999): 335–51.

Fagan, B. *The Little Ice Age: How Climate Made History, 1300–1850.* New York: Basic Books, 2000.

Shindell, D.T., G.A. Schmidt, M.E. Mann, D. Rind, and A. Waple. "Solar Forcing of Regional Climate Change during the Maunder Minimum." *Science* 294 (2001): 2149–52.

Stahle, D.W., M.K. Cleaveland, D.B. Blanton, M.D. Therrell, and D.A. Gay. "The Lost Colony and Jamestown Droughts." *Science* 280 (1998): 564–67.

Volcanoes: A Chilling Fury

Ambrose, S.H. "Late Pleistocene Human Population Bottlenecks, Volcanic Winter, and Differentiation of Modern Humans." *Journal of Human Evolution* 34 (1998): 623–51.

Briffa, K.R., P.D. Jones, F.H. Schweingruber, and T.J. Osborn. "Influence of Volcanic Eruptions on Northern Hemisphere Summer Temperature over the Past 600 Years." *Nature* 393 (1998): 450–55.

Stommel, H.M., and E. Stommel. *Volcano Weather: The Story of 1816, the Year without a Summer.* New York: Simon and Schuster, 1983.

Stothers, R.B. "Climatic and Demographic Consequences of the Massive Volcanic Eruption of 1258." *Climatic Change* 45 (2000): 361–74.

Zeilinga de Boer, J., and D.T. Sanders. *Volcanoes in Human History: The Far-Reaching Effects of Major Eruptions.* Princeton: Princeton University Press, 2001.

El Niño: The Child's Tantrums

Caviedes, C.N. *El Niño in History: Storming through the Ages.* Gainesville: University Press of Florida, 2001.

Fagan, B. *Floods, Famines, and Emperors: El Niño and the Fate of Civilizations.* New York: Basic Books, 1999.

Grove, R. "Global Impact of the 1789–93 El Niño." *Nature* 393 (1998): 318–19.

Kumar, K.K., B. Rajagopalan, M. Hoerling, G. Bates, and M. Cane. "Unraveling the Mystery of Indian Monsoon Failure during El Niño." *Science* 314 (2006): 115–19.

McPhaden, M.J. "El Niño: The Child Prodigy of 1997–98." *Nature* 398 (1999): 559–62.

War: Skies of Rage

Brönnimann, S., J. Luterbacher, J. Staehelin, T.M. Svendby, G. Hansen, and T. Svenøe. "Extreme Climate of the Global Troposphere and Stratosphere in 1940–42 Related to El Niño." *Nature* 431 (2004): 971–74.

Durschmied, E. *The Weather Factor: How Nature Has Changed History.* London: Hodder and Stoughton, 2000.

Faris, S. "The Real Roots of Darfur." *Atlantic Monthly* 299 (2007): 67–69.

Hyslop, S.G., J. Newton, and H. Woodward, eds. *The Third Reich: Barbarossa.* Alexandria, VA: Time-Life Books, 1990.

Zhang, D.D., P. Brecke, H.F. Lee, Y. He, and J. Zhang. "Global Climate Change, War, and Population Decline in Recent Human History." *Proceedings of the National Academy of Sciences* 104 (2007): 19214-19.

Weathering the Future

Bradshaw, W.E., and C.M. Holzapfel. "Evolutionary Response to Rapid Climate Change." *Science* 312 (2006): 1477–78.

Fekri, A.H. "A River Runs through Egypt: Nile Floods and Civilization." *Geotimes* 50 (2005): 22–25.

Flannery, T. *The Weather Makers.* Toronto: HarperCollins, 2005.

Hansen, J., M. Sato, R. Ruedy, K. Lo, D.W. Lea, and M. Medina-Elizade. "Global Temperature Change." *Proceedings of the National Academy of Sciences* 103 (2007): 14288–93.

Intergovernmental Panel on Climate Change. *Climate Change 2007: Impacts, Adaptation and Vulnerability.* Cambridge: Cambridge University Press, 2007.

INDEX

PHOTO CREDITS

Maps by Antonia Banyard. Background textures © istockphoto.com/ Peter Zelei (parchment) and © istockphoto.com/Shawn Gearhart. Basic outlines by Map Resources.

15 LC-USZC2-2887; **37** LC-M32-965; **41** LC-M32-289; **42** LOT 11356- 28; **48** Illus in AP2.H32 1875 (Case Y); **51** POS-TH-1895.R86, no. 2 (C size); **55** U.S. GEOG FILE - Hawaii –Industry; **76** Illus. in E141.B88 1970; **93** Illus. in AP2.H32 1883 (Case Y); **108** LC-M32- 52465-x; **112** LOT 11640-F; **113** LC-B22-335-4; **116** LC-B2-4028-14; **119** BIOG FILE – Robespierre, Maximilien François Marie Isidore de, 1758–1794; **121** LOT 10484. All courtesy of the Library of Congress Prints and Photographs Division.

18 The Art Archive; **33** The Art Archive/Archaeolgical Museum Baghdad/ Gianni Dagli Orti; **66** The Art Archive; **96** The Art Archive/Gianni Dagli Orti; **115** The Art Archive/National Maritime Museum London/Harper Collins Publishers.

22, 86, 90, 92. All courtesy of United States Geological Survey, United States Department of Interior.

27 and **80.** Graphics by Irvin Cheung.

27 (globe photo), **75, 107.** Courtesy of NASA.

10 © Mike Page; **11** © istockphoto.com/Alexander Hafemann; **13** © istockphoto.com/Pauline Mills; **14** © istockphoto.com/Mike Bentley; **19** © Wessex Archaeology, used with permission; **21** © Narcis Parfenti/ www.sxc.hu; **23** © istockphoto.com/Fanelie Rosier; **25** © istockphoto. com/Konstantin Tovstiadi; **26** © istockphoto.com; **35** © istockphoto. com/Volker Kreinacke; **40** © Colleen MacMillan, used with permission; **44** © istockphoto.com; **46** © istockphoto.com /Robert Churchill; **49,** courtesy of NASA/National Optical Astronomy Observatory; **52** © istockphoto.com /Denise Kappa; **53** © istockphoto.com; **57** © istockphoto.com/David Hughes; **58** © istockphoto.com/Hsing- Wen Hsu; **60** © istockphoto.com/Nancy Nehring; **64** © istockphoto.com/ Jillian Pond; **65** © istockphoto.com/Steve Dibblee; **69** © istockphoto.com/ Ian Ilott; **73** © istockphoto.com/Enkhtamir Enkhdavaa; **81** © istockphoto. com/Cristina Ciochina; **83** © istockphoto.com/Photo by Hulton Archive/ Getty Images; **89** © istockphoto.com/Jarno Gonzalez Zarraonandia;

ACKNOWLEDGMENTS

I would like to thank Dr. John Smol, professor of paleolimnology at Queen's University, Ontario, and Dr. Laird Christie, emeritus professor of anthropology at Wilfrid Laurier University, Ontario, for their review of the material in this book and for their comments and suggestions. I am especially grateful to Elizabeth McLean, an outstanding and encouraging editor whose work made this book possible. My thanks to Antonia Banyard, Audrey McClellan, and Irvin Cheung for putting this together. And, as always, thanks to Priscilla, Laura, and Hannah for their support and patience.

ABOUT THE AUTHOR

Peter Christie is a science writer and editor whose previous books for children, *Naturally Wild Musicians* and *Well-Schooled Fish and Feathered Bandits*, explore the science of animal behavior. He lives in Kingston, Ontario, with his wife and their two daughters.